Congrat
winnie,
2013) PCPC
Tom Lamar Cory Ch...

THOSE
SOUTHERN
LAMARS

THOSE SOUTHERN LAMARS

*The Stories
of Five Illustrious Lamars*

Thomas Lamar Coughlin

To order additional copies of this book, contact:
Xlibris Corporation
1-888-7-XLIBRIS
www.Xlibris.com
Orders@Xlibris.com

CONTENTS

This work is dedicated to the many Lamar family members who have been helpful. Specifically I would like to thank Gerry Hunter, G.Lamar Crittenden, Jeb Patch, Lamar Washington and Howard Robert Lamar.

INTRODUCTION

My desire to turn the dry facts of genealogy and land records into tales of the places, people and things to which I and my readers can relate has lead me to compiling the real-life stories that are written here.

Like my father before me, I was born in a Depression-stricken Massachusetts textile mill city. Fall River which clung to a bayside slope overlooking Narragansett Bay, between New Bedford and Providence, Rhode Island, and directly north of Newport. My Yankee father had won the hand of a Southern belle, and after working and living in Chicago and New York, he brought her home to his native Massachusetts in the mid-1930s.

Six years later I was born, early in the year that history books remember for Pearl Harbor. Mother had been born in her family's native Maryland in the early days of this century and had grown up in nearby Washington, D.C. She is a ninth-generation Marylander and thus had an abundance of family members always about as she grew up. As a young girl she had been fortunate to hear stories that had been told, first hand, by senior family members who had been born before the Civil War. These stories detailed family events that took place in the period immediately before and during that war, while some were even older. Years later, when I heard those old tales, I found them absolutely spellbinding. I was most impressed by the fact that they came to me only one person removed from the original, long-since-deceased story tellers. Because I viewed the Civil War as having happened in the distant past and knew it to be of such paramount importance in the history of our country, I was enthralled by them. It was a great surprise to discover true-life stories of family members from earlier days and this naturally increased my interest in my own mother's Southern family, of which I had learned too little while growing up. I soon learned of letters and other papers of my deceased aunt. The genealogy was all there—in desk drawers and in libraries, printed in black and white, having been researched and written long ago. The only trouble was that too much of it consisted of little more than birth and death dates—the "begats."

I knew from the genealogical records that the first of Mother's family to come to this country was Thomas Lamar, who is reported to have come into Maryland in the 1660s from Virginia, on his way from either France or England. These dry facts lacked the real-life stories and day-to-day detail about the lives of those ancestors between birth and death. In contrast, Mother's tales were about the lives of people who seemed to almost come alive in my mind's eye, a bit like characters in a novel. I became convinced that those people of the old dusty records, my ancestors, would become more real and understandable to me only when I could learn something about what their daily lives had been like.

To find more of the wonderful stories of those ancestors, I embarked on a mission to learn as much as I could of the lives and goings on of the members of what my mother had so often described as her—Large Old Southern Family." I had started to learn something more about the Lamars in a somewhat haphazard fashion from typewritten notes made by one of my aunts, but it wasn't until a chance meeting in the 1970s with the then-head of the technology transfer office at Massachusetts Institute of Technology, a wonderful man named Lamar Washington, that the curtain of doubt and mystery was pulled aside. A book that he showed me confirmed that the more famous Lamars about whom several books had been written—Lucius Quintus Cincinnatus (L.Q.C.) Lamar and Mirabeau Buonaparte Lamar—were descended from the same Thomas Lamar of Maryland that my mother's records showed. This discovery opened the door to a treasure trove of Lamar family stories. The pictures painted by these stories include an 1830s steamship disaster in which the steamship-owner/father witnessed the loss of his wife and all of his children except his oldest son. Another story paints the picture of an Army private on horseback in 1836. On the eve of a major battle, he gallops into a group of enemy soldiers to save the life of the Texas Secretary of War. As a result, he was immediately promoted from private to colonel and the next day, at the victorious battle of San Jacinto, his name became forever etched in Texas history. Yet another is about buying and equipping Civil War blockade-runners sailing out of Bermuda through the Union blockade into Wilmington, North Carolina.

I discovered that the history of the Lamar family in the United States is a long and intricate tale of early immigrants who were able to establish themselves in the New World in the late 1600s, and then went on to gain large landholdings that increased in the following centuries. Thomas, the—Father Abraham" of the family whose will was probated in 1714, left his two sons, Thomas and John, extensive tracts of land. Those inherited land holdings were expanded by the younger Thomas, and after his death a family meeting was held by his heirs to plan for the future. As a result, five of the eight children of the younger Thomas chose to leave Maryland and to pioneer newly opened lands in the Deep South. The other three stayed in Maryland, at least for a while, where they prospered and continued the family line. Several of the family members who moved to the new lands in the South were among the earliest settlers there, and for that reason several towns there were named after the Lamar family, along with counties in four different states.

One branch of the family, following (and perhaps because of) the intermarriage of first cousins, produced sons who went on to gain great distinction. One of those sons became that hero of the Republic of Texas and later its president. Another was a brilliant young legal scholar who committed suicide in the family garden on the Fourth of July at the outset of a brilliant career. His son and namesake went on to become a senator and was one of two Lamars to sit on the Supreme Court of the United States. The family has had the misfortune to have produced sons who were casualties in all of this nation's wars, beginning at least with the American Revolution, but most notably in our bloody Civil War. Members of the family on both sides of that conflict offered the ultimate sacrifice, with the greatest number fighting under the Stars and Bars of the Confederacy. In his *Profiles in Courage,* John F. Kennedy wrote: "Of the thirteen descendants of the first Lamar in America who served in the Confederate Armies with the rank of Lieutenant Colonel or above, seven perished in the war."

Very early land records show that the spelling of the family name in those early days varied from deed to deed, almost certainly based on the tastes, knowledge and spelling abilities of the clerk charged with recording the facts related to any given land transaction. Some of these variations include Lamore, Lemur, Lamaire, and De La Maire. Although family correspondence indicates an early choice of the current spelling Lamar, *The History of the Lamar and Lemar Family in America* by Harold Dihel Lemar (published in Omaha, Nebraska, in 1941) offers conclusive evidence that Lamar was not the only way that members have decided to spell the family name. That book tells us that John Lamar, son of the founding father Thomas, had a son Charles who ended up spelling the family name as—Lemar." The fact that two spellings occurred within the same family, who lived in the same state, if not the same county, would indicate that the Americanized versions differed from the French original. Cate, the author of a biography of L.Q.C. Lamar, tells us that the original name was Lamore, and that part of the family remained in England using the name Delamare. If this is true, the name Lamar as now found in the United States is almost always derived from the heirs of Thomas and John Lamar, as Peter had no male heirs.

Certainly the vast majority of the descendants of this family were regular, everyday folks. Most were farmers, especially in the family's early years in America. A small number, however, including the Georgia-pioneer-turned-Texas hero, went on to gain fame, if not notoriety. Of the two sons the family produced who sat on the Supreme Court, Lucius Quintus Cincinnatus Lamar is rightly celebrated in John F. Kennedy's *Profiles in Courage* for taking political stands that he knew were correct but unpopular.

The fame or notoriety of these few and well known family members resulted in more towns being named after the Lamar family. In Texas, a county was named after Mirabeau Buonaparte Lamar, who had the good sense and fortune to show up at the battle of San Jacinto, which the Texans won, rather than at Goliad or the ill-fated defense of the Alamo. In all, a total of eighteen towns in the following states are named Lamar: Alabama, Arkansas, Colorado, Georgia, Indiana, Kansas, Louisiana, Mississippi, Missouri, Nebraska, Oklahoma, Pennsylvania, South Carolina, Washington, Wisconsin, West Virginia—and two towns in Texas. Lamar, Colorado was so named by the town fathers in the futile hope of receiving a United States mining office. They tried to influence the placement of the government office through flattery by naming their Colorado town Lamar while L.Q.C. Lamar just happened to be Secretary of the Interior during Cleveland's presidency. That flattery didn't work, and some other town was selected to house the mining office. Also, there are counties named Lamar in Texas, Mississippi (in addition to the town), Georgia, and Alabama. There is also a Lamar River in Yellowstone National Park.

One son of the then-quite-large and well dispersed family was a real "Black Sheep" who gained quite a measure of notoriety before the Civil War. That notoriety has been renewed, years after his reckless and futile death in the waning days of an already lost war. This Black Sheep was Charles Augustus Lafayette Lamar, a colonel in the Confederate Army who died in a vain and useless firefight against Federal troops who were attempting to cross the bridge over the Chattahoochee River outside Columbus, Georgia. Lee had already capitulated, and his Army of Northern Virginia was already on its way home from Appomattox Court House; the war was clearly lost when the young man died.

This Charles Lamar had been raised in ante-bellum Georgia, where the owning of slaves was common and legal. In 1808, however, importation of additional slaves had been outlawed by the Constitution. But as a member of a large group of families that both owned slaves and accepted slave owning as a daily reality, Charles Lamar invested, along with his friends and some relatives, in one or more sailing ships purchased to run the blockade and bring in new slaves. Years after the Civil War and his death, Charles Lamar's blockade running activities came to public attention in great detail when his personal letter books were discovered moments before they were to be recycled into new paper at a New England paper mill. A college student working summers noticed these letter books, and upon reading them decided that they should be saved. Subsequent publication of these books in the *North American Review* in 1886 has insured that virtually every book about slavery in the United States has related the exploits of Charles A.L. Lamar in fascinating detail. The stories in these diaries are bold tales documenting an appalling traffic in human beings, a traffic that was so much a part of the history of the ante-bellum South. These diaries don't focus on, or indeed make much reference at all to, the poor conditions that the human cargo had to suffer or their fate upon delivery. They concentrate on the financial, administrative, business and anecdotal sides of what was just another business venture. Recently, a friend I have known for years in Massachusetts, upon hearing that I had a Lamar connection, told me that his grandmother was a Lamar and that he had an old family bible in his possession. I was amazed when I learned that the old Bible turned out to be that of Charles A.L. Lamar.

Another story about Charles' exploits was told years after the war by an old man who claimed to have been an investor in Charles Lamar's blockade runner, *Wanderer*. He spun a tale that claimed that Charles A.L. Lamar hosted a dinner dance for the crew of a Federal fort to distract them, allowing *Wanderer* to slip past the fort, which guarded the river channel near Savannah. The story goes that the social activities were timed to cause the fort's crew to be looking away from the river at a time during peak tide when the ship slipped past. Recently, the author of a contemporary book about *Wanderer*'s exploits casts serious doubts on the old man's recollection of that event. Nonetheless, the story has been published in several books on slavery. These books can be found on many library shelves, thus insuring that the questionable tale lives on.

Another Lamar famous in his nineteenth century day, in spite of a very strange- sounding name, was Gazaway Bugg Lamar. A tycoon on a grand scale, he was a successful businessman and banker as well as the father of Charles, the blockade-running slaver. After establishing himself as a cotton broker and steamship operator in Savannah, Georgia (he owned the steamship on which his wife and much of his family ultimately perished), he later moved to New York, where among his various ventures, he founded and ran the Bank of the Republic. Just before the Civil War broke out, he was able to help the Southern cause on several occasions. Once he actually bought small arms for the State of Georgia from the United States Armory, quite openly and legally. He also arranged to have Confederate bonds printed in New York, since engravers with the necessary skills to do the job didn't exist the South. When the Civil War finally broke out he returned to Georgia and worked there in support of the Confederate government. As part of that effort, he later formed The Importing and Exporting Company of Georgia to run cotton and other goods through the blockade. Finally, when Sherman's troops occupied Savannah, Gazaway B. Lamar took steps to save all that he could by accepting an invitation issued by the Federal military governor which called for the residents of Savannah to take an oath in accord with President Lincoln's proclamation of December 8, 1863. That proclamation promised to guarantee the restoration of property rights to those Southerners swearing adherence to the Constitution of the United States. Lamar decided that the best course was "to take the oath to support it [the Constitution], and abide by the proclamation concerning slavery, and be restored to all *f* rights of property except slaves."

Gazaway believed that taking the oath would protect his substantial assets, but the carpetbaggers and the political climate in the occupied South almost caused him to lose it all. After seemingly endless legal proceedings, Gazaway was finally awarded a settlement of almost $600,000. Although this was only half of the amount originally claimed, this was the largest individual award of the post-war period . He had fought and won a heroic and protracted legal battle for his property, but Gazaway B. Lamar died in 1874 only six months after receiving the settlement.

The Lamar name is often used as a first name and sometimes indicates membership in the family descending from Thomas Lamar, but the name is color blind. African American families named Lamar would most probably have taken the name upon emancipation, indicating that their families had been slaves on Lamar-owned plantations. One well-known person, the movie actress Hedi Lamarr, was not related to the Lamar family at all. She was actually born in what used to be Czechoslovakia with a completely different name, and the name Lamarr was picked for her by producers.

While the seventeenth century saw the establishment of the Lamar family in America, and the eighteenth century saw the growth and movement of the family across much of the South, family members experienced their greatest public achievements in the nineteenth century. Mirabeau Buonaparte Lamar, Gazaway Bugg Lamar, and Henry Graybill Lamar were born in 1798. The other subjects of this book who were to achieve fame in the new century were born in the nineteenth century, and almost all of them died before 1900.

My own first success in turning dry facts and minimal historic information into something tangible began with my search for the location of Thomas Lamar's initial residence, a Maryland plantation with the idyllic name "The Fishing Place" in Prince Georges County, Maryland (which had originally been part of Calvert County). This was a tidewater tobacco growing homestead on the Patuxent River, just north of the Potomac. I began with only the information contained in the original deed. This scant information turned out to be most helpful and necessary in helping me to

locate The Fishing Place. The ancient document told me that two
of the boundaries were the Patuxent River and Trent Creek. The
Patuxent River is large enough to be on very large-scale maps, but
the same cannot be said for the creek. Investigation and good luck
led me in the early 1980s to a kindly soul at the U.S. Geological
Service in Washington. He told me whom to call to find a book
listing all of Maryland's rivers and creeks. Alas, Trent Creek was
not listed, but a Trent Hall Creek that flowed into the Patuxent
was. This similar name begged for further investigation, especially
as it was located near St. Mary's City, the state's earliest settlement. In addition this was the only name that even came close to
what I was looking for. Maryland Route 5 leads through the town
of Mechanicsville, which had been identified by my contact in the
Geological Service as the nearest town of consequence.

After passing through Mechanicsville, heading south, away
from Washington, I arbitrarily chose the next road on the left (as I
study my computer maps years later I believe it could be Route
6), heading east toward the river. On a guess, I then turned left on
to a little back country road that ran parallel to the river. When a
small road soon appeared on the right, I had already made the
arbitrary decision not to turn there but instead I would just read
the street sign and drive on past. As I read the name of the street,
however, I immediately jammed on the brakes: the sign read Trent
Hall Creek Road. Traveling down this road toward the river, the
rough and hilly countryside soon gave way to flat and fertile tidewater farmland, and a vista that lay before me had the appearance
and feeling of having been unchanged from long ago.

Corn fields lined both sides of the road leading to a very gra-
cious, riverfront brick home several hundred years old. An elderly
black man was driving a tractor along the road. I yelled, "Excuse
me, can you . . ." "trying to be heard over the noise of the engine.
Finally I caught his eye; the engine slowed, and the noise died.
"Could you tell me if . . ." "No, suh, I can't help you, but if you
talk to the Missus in that house down by the river, she can answer
your question" was the reply that I received. At the end of the road

was that stately old brick home, with its beautiful, well-kept lawn stretching down to the river. It looked like an inspiration for a Currier and Ives print. After knocking on the door and calling repeatedly with no response, I knocked yet again and finally entered the kitchen. Still with no response, I gingerly entered the dining room, calling "HELLO" as loudly as seemed right. Finally a response came from upstairs.

Although I feared meeting some frightened woman holding a shotgun, the lady of the house was very cheerful as she entered the room. Well dressed yet casual, she was in her sixties. The years had been kind as she had retained a substantial amount of the good looks she had been blessed with in her youth. I told her who I was and what had brought me to her house. Quickly, she understood my mission and was more than happy to tell me the story of Trent Hall. After a brief search, she pulled out an album that contained, among other mementos, a copy of the original deed. Sure enough, the description told me that this land was bounded by the Patuxent River and Trent Creek. When the house in which we found ourselves had been built, it had been named Trent Hall, apparently after the creek that bounded the property. Over the years the creek for which the house had originally been named had come to be known by the name of the house. Now I understood that Trent Hall Creek and Trent Creek were one and the same, and I realized that I was finally walking the land trod by my ancient ancestor, Thomas Lamar. Or so I thought until I rechecked and saw that while Thomas Lamar's house had been on the north side of the creek, we were on the south side! The day was getting late, and the hundred-mile-plus drive back to Washington started to look very long. When my hostess told me that the driving distance to the other side of the narrow creek was almost 20 miles and that the old house that had been over there, which she thought was not as old as Trent Hall, had been torn down years before, I quickly made the decision to accept this wonderful old Trent Hall as my mind's-eye picture of The Fishing Place. Certainly, Thomas Lamar had walked on this land and the view of the river was the very same that he had viewed. It was the same river where he had fished and sailed. I knew that I had finally found exactly what I had set out to find. Eureka!

Anyone wishing to find the location of The Fishing Place should go to Golden Beach, Maryland, which is a small waterfront subdivision on the Patuxent, just north of Trent (Hall) Creek. To find it, go about three miles south of Hughesville, and look for Golden Beach Road on the left. Follow it to the water—since the original grant was for fifty acres you should be at the site of original plantation most anywhere in the subdivision, especially at the river's edge.

1

THE PIONEERS

To understand why a Frenchman would choose Maryland as a place to settle in the seventeenth century rather than Virginia or another colony requires an appreciation of what may have been an immigrant's motivation, along with a little knowledge of the laws of property ownership in those days. While it is hard to estimate with much accuracy what the true motivation was behind Thomas Lamar's coming to America (although there have been claims that that Lamars were Huguenots fleeing religious prosecution), we do know something about the laws of that day. Prior to 1649, the law in the English colonies in America barred non-Englishmen from owning land. That law was changed in 1649, when Lord Baltimore invited Frenchmen, Germans and other Europeans to come to the Maryland colony. He offered them property rights including, among other things, free land and all other rights that previously had been limited to Englishmen. Most likely that offer by Lord Baltimore influenced the decision of Thomas Lamar to come to America. It is certain that after immigrating his material success in America was substantial, as attested to by the land holdings he amassed prior to the time of his death. It is hard to imagine that someone with that much drive to accumulate property would have been willing to come to a colony in certain knowledge that he would be a second-class citizen, unable to own property. The land records show that on September 14, 1663 the Maryland Provincial Assembly approved a petition from Thomas and Peter "Lamore" for naturalization. The title of the petition refers to "Pattents of

Dennizacon to Thomas Lamore and Peter Lamore of french de-
scent." Subsequently, Lord Baltimore granted a certificate (now
on record in Annapolis) that states

> Whereas Thomas and Peter Lamore, late of Virginia, and
> subjects of the crown of France, having transported them-
> selves into this province here to abide, have besought us to
> grant them, the said Thomas and Peter Lamore, leave to
> inhabit here as free denizens, and freedom land to them and
> their heirs to purchase,
> Know ye, that we, willingly to give encouragement to the
> subjects of that crown, do hereby declare them, the said
> Thomas and Peter Lamore, to be free denizens of this our
> province of Maryland . . .

Next we find that on November 24, 1665, Thomas petitioned for
a land grant to be indemnified for transporting himself and his
wife Mary into the province. That petition was granted on the
same day that it was submitted. The land records, as well as his
will, show him to be a successful planter.

As to why Thomas Lamar left Europe or why he found the
attraction of a new land so compelling, we are forced to guess.
Certainly, Colonial America in the latter half of the 1600s was still
quite a primitive place, with few settlers. Land was cheap and plen-
tiful, and with even a modest amount of money, an amount inad-
equate to purchase substantial land holdings in Europe, an ambi-
tious immigrant was able to purchase and accumulate a very substantial amount of land in colonial Maryland. Thomas Lamar's
original properties came from "headright" grants offered as incen-
tives to enter the new land, and over the years he was able to add
to his holdings.

The Maryland tidewater was fertile ground for growing tobacco, a crop that proved to be profitable due both to increasing
demand and to the fact that this crop wouldn't grow just anywhere. The continued purchasing of land by Thomas Lamar was

most probably funded substantially, if not totally, by profits from this crop. As is true with any agricultural activity, the profitability of growing tobacco was sometimes good and at other times bad. Around 1660 tobacco was worth 14 shillings per hundred weight, but by 1666 the price was down to just over seven. The idea of withholding some land from cultivation and cut the crop by 50% the next year with the goal of increasing the price gained some support. But this price increase never came to pass in the manner envisioned by the planters. Mother Nature intervened in the form of a hurricane, and after two days of gales, rain and hail, three-quarters of the Maryland tobacco crop was lost. The strong upward pressure this put on prices for the next two years eliminated any further talk of limiting crop size as an economic strategy.

Among his several plantations, Thomas Lamar took The Fishing Place for his homestead. As is typical of these early deeds, the wording is very inexact and flowery when compared to modern documents, which need to be precise and detailed. The deed to that Plantation includes both interesting payment terms as well as boundary descriptions:

> Charles, Absolute Lord and Proprietary of the province of Maryland and Avalon Lord Baron of Baltimore, &c.
>
> To all persons to whom these presents shall come, Greetings in our Lord God Everlasting. Know ye that we for and in consideration that Thomas LaMare of Calvert County in our said province of Maryland hath due unto him fifty acres of land within our Province . . . upon such conditions and terms as are expressed in the Conditions of Plantation of our late father Cecelius of noble memory under his greater seal at Arms bearing date at London the second day of July of our Lord 1649 . . .
>
> Do hereby grant unto him the said Thomas LaMare all the parcel of land called The Fishing Place situate lying and being in Calvert County on the West side of Patuxent River and North side of Trent Creek . . . To have and to hold the

same unto him the said Thomas La Mare, his heirs and assigns forever-to be holden of us and our heirs at our receipt of St. Marries at the two most usual feasts of the year, viz: at the feast of the Annunciation of the Blessed Virgin Mary and the feast of St. Michael the Arch Angel by even and equal portions the Rent of two Shilling Sterling in Silver or Gold.

Given at our city of St. Marries under the great seal of our said Province of Maryland the fifth day of April in the second year of our dominion over our said Province Annoque Dam. . . . One Thousand Six hundred seventy seven.

With all the plantations he had to manage, it is hard to imagine Thomas doing much leisurely fishing, but it is safe to guess that he found men to help him work his properties.

Records from the Johnston family collection in the Maryland Historical Society indicate that Thomas and Mary had one son, also named Thomas, who was born in 1682. After the death of his first wife, Mary, Thomas wed again (to Ann Pottinger), but details of his domestic life are scarce. Records show that Thomas and Ann had a son John, born in 1693. A 1701 deed signed by Thomas and Ann Lamar establishes that this second marriage had taken place by that date. While the data is interesting, and possibly correct, there no clue as to who recorded the dates or where their information came from.

Ann Pottinger Lamar survived Thomas and was made his executrix. The will, which was probated in 1714, indicates that he may have owned property in England, or possibly he had bank accounts there. The document states

I give unto my well beloved son, Thomas LaMar, the plantation on which he now dwelled with half of the land which I now possess to him and his heirs forever. I give unto my well beloved son John LaMar, the plantation on which I now dwell with half of the land to him and his heirs forever.

It is my will that my well beloved wife enjoy all my land and movable estate both here and in England, during her widowhood. If my beloved wife marry before her decease, the removable estate should be divided into three parts: Thomas one part; John, one part; leaving my wife her third wholly at her disposal. I leave unto the priest, Mr. Lurell, five hundred pounds of good clean tobacco. Witness my hand and seal 4th October, 1712.

The witnesses to the will were John Pettinger, Samuel Pettinger, and John Turner. Thomas the Elder is believed to have been buried at or near The Fishing Place.

His sons, John and Thomas the younger increased their estates. Thomas was reported to be among the most influential planters of the province. His plantations, in the fashion of later Southern plantations or Texas cattle ranches, were given names. Some of those—named in his will—were wonderfully descriptive, but others have meaning only for people long since deceased: "Conclusion," "The Pines," "Two Brothers," "Valentine's Garden," "Joseph and James," and "Hunting Hill." Some of these were reported to be along Rock Creek and Muddy Branch, both familiar names around the nation's capital. Of these, "Hunting Hill" is especially interesting, for the reason that to this day there is a large farmhouse surrounded by many acres named Hunting Hill. It is in the area near Rockville, on Travilah Road in North Potomac, and the general area is now known by the name "Hunting Hill." It is possible that this farm is what is left of the younger Thomas Lamar's "Hunting Hill."

John Lamar moved inland to the Frederick Valley, where his sons John Jr. and Robert LaMar patented a 2017-acre tract of land near Middle Creek in 1755 called Wells Invention. Unfortunately, John Lamar Jr. died the next year, and his only son, William Bishop Lamar, was just a boy of about twelve years of age. A mortgage on the property ("along with sundry negro slaves") had been given to one Bryan Philpot, a merchant from London. Philpot sold the mortgage in 1760. At that time in Maryland a law was on the books that allowed an infant to redeem mortgaged property any time within twenty years after coming of age. So in 1785 William Bishop Lamar, after having served in the Revolutionary War, sued the heirs of the man who had bought Wells Invention. The suit demanded that he be allowed to redeem the mortgage. Initially, the lawsuit was denied in court and the case went to the appellate court. There the case was found to have merit, and after winning the appeal William Bishop Lamar was allowed to redeem his inherited land. He did just that, and in the early 1800s he sold part of it, named "Resurvey of Wells Invention," to his son (yet another) Thomas.

Thomas LaMar the younger left six sons and two married daughters to inherit his extensive holdings. This group of heirs continued to live on the inherited lands for seven years after their father's death. But by 1755 the land was becoming exhausted from the continual raising of tobacco. Family members met and, responding to the call of opportunity, decided to sell the Maryland holdings and remove to new lands. Brothers Robert, Thomas, John, and Samuel, along with their brother-in-law Clementius Davis, husband of Mary Lamar, packed up children, animals, and slaves and moved to the newly opening lands to the south. The stories of productive land at attractive prices must have appealed to those sons and daughters of a large family, many of whom had large families of their own. Two remaining brothers and the other brother-in-law, not as strongly attracted by the promise of the new southern lands, decided to remain in Maryland. While no written records are known to have survived that document that family meeting, it is safe to speculate that there was a fair amount of discussion over the decision to leave well-established plantations, friends, and extended family. They would be departing a region they had grown up in, knew well, and probably loved for the unknowns of a new locale.

Many members of the family ended up in Georgia, which until 1752 had been administered by a board of trustees. In 1751, when the British Parliament had refused to allocate additional money to the trustees, they forfeited their charter, which was scheduled to expire in any case, in June of 1753. Also forfeited were trustees' land rights. Because the British Crown was well versed in governing colonies, they took over administering the affairs of the colony from the trustees, and by 1755 land was being granted by the colonial government to settlers at no cost save a charge for surveying and office fees. The head of each family received 150 acres, and another 50 acres was awarded for each additional member of the household, including slaves and indentured servants. More land could be claimed as the family grew or as slaves were added. In the first decade of royal government almost 400,000 acres of land were granted, and in the second decade almost 800,000. Efforts were made to insure that settlers would clear and work the land to deter speculators and absentee landlords.

A move of that distance, from Maryland to Georgia, was sure to put stress on Lamar family ties. We are able to catch a glimpse of that hardship from several family letters. One, from the Lamar records of the Maryland Historical Society, appears to be from Thomas Lamar (III), who had moved south, to his brother-in-law, Joseph Wilson (who was married to Thomas' sister Elizabeth). Thomas wrote

> Sir:
> John Lamar intends to be in Maryland this fall by whom you will have an opportunity of sending me an answer on the occasion within mentioned.
> N. B. Mother desires to be remembered to you and your spouse and to cousin Molly and all the children in the most affectionate loving manner, and says she should be extremely glad to hear often from you as she never expects to see any of you more in this world. My brothers likewise send their particular respects to you and family.

Another letter, which had been in the possession of a Mrs. Irvin of

Athens, Georgia, in the 1930s, was from Joseph Wilson to Thomas and the other Lamars:

> Maryland Frederick County,
> Crabbs Hall, on Vallintines
> Garden on Rock Creek,
> Oct. 28, 1770

Dear Friends

I take this opportunity of wrighting once more to you, notwithstanding you seem to have quite forgot and forsaken us; as I have not received a letter from you of you since the 22d of June 1767; which was from my loving kinsman Robt Lamar—since which I have sent many, thou know not whether they may have come to hand or not, as I have not received any accounts that may be depended on from any of you. I well remember that I have complained of your short letters, but should be extremely glad of a short one rather than none at all. This is to acquaint you we are in reasonable good health at present my wife only excepted, who is much troubled with a choackeing & sudden cold & hot fits and changes in her—hope this will find you in good health on your receipt hereof. I have been fully determined in my mind, with God's permission, to have been out with you this fall,—but find it out of my power. I know not whether that Day may ever be when I shall see you more on this side the grave; I have just made good Contract signed on last march with Mr. Alexander Urquhart brother to Peter heir to the Parson for all his lands bought from you the Lamars except what he had before sold; I have contracted with him for Oald Mr. T. Lamar's Dwelling plantation containing 300 acres: Robt, Thos, John & Saml Lamar Dwelling plantations containing 992 1/2 acres, the whole containing Twelve hundred ninety two & a half acres at twenty shillings Ster. per acre. I reserve to myself the Oald plantation also five hundred acres of the other including Thos &

John Lamar plantation which extends into Robts plantation the remainder with Robts and Samls plantations including Zac—Magruder has at the same price. I veryly
beleave I could on saying the word only, have for the part I
hold at least Twenty Five Shills Sterl pr acre, if not thirty
paid down. A most surprising change in the value of lands;
and still growing—I seem quite out of the notion of moving
with my family at present as I grow in years and no son
capable to take the burden off my hands; we have had very
good prices for our Tobacco & Wheat for this three or four
years past. Crops of Cyder occasioned by the later Spring
frosts to be very short this several years past. Which helps
keep our Spritis a little down—I think my family since Sistr
Sarah Lamar Departure for hence has increased fifteen in
number; besides my Daughter Mary two children the El-
dest a daughter which is Dead the other a son, we have one
child only since; which is a son whom was two years old the
7th of Augt last and can't speak one word yet, he still sucks
the bobey he has been an aldening child but how has got to
be a hearty fellow. We have had ten negro children born
since, two of which is dead and six grown negroes I bought
at two hundred & five pounds Ster. Know that my family
exclusive of my Son-in-law and Daughter Mary and family
contains the number of thirty and three. Quite too large a
family to move so far with. I still flatter myself I shall come
out once more in order to do something with my land on
Beach Island, tho think not to fix upon a home any more till
they near ready to start for the Journey—Should be glad to
hear how it stands whether Clear or Lumbered, hope the
use of it or Rents of it may keep it clear of the taxes & Quit
rents as it may one Day or other be of service to my children,
if not to me. I hope Dear Friends you wont delay wrighting
as you have done. I intend to miss no opportunity & hope
you wont.

This I hope will serve as a visit to you all my Friends though may be not so sattisfactory as in person. Yet it may serve to keep up our memoriall of each other, as we have no other way of doing it at present being so far severed one from the other. The God of Heaven I hope will grant us a happy meeting in the Day of our Lord.

I am Dear Brother Sisters and relations all, your most affectionate sincear well wisher & am in Joynt Love with my spouse your Brother-in-law.

[signed]

Joseph Wilson

PS. As it is impossible to direct one letter to you All my friends & the uncertainty of the comeing to hand hope I shall stand excused and it meet with the same kind of reception as if directed to all of you my old friends andrelations. Mr Peter Young's wife is dead. J. W. Little thought I when we parted in Virginia on your way out we should not have met before this time if life lasted, but there is no accounting for these things. Man appoints and God disappoints. To Sistr Sarah & Sons

[Address on above] to Messs Thomas Lamar, Senr and Sarah Lamar & Sons liveing in South Carolinas on Savanah River Nowwinsder Township in Granvile County near the mouth of Horse Creek. Favr of Mr James Lee. These with care.

The pain of removal and the loss of loved ones to time and distance continued to affect Lamars into the nineteenth century. These themes are sounded in a letter written on March 23, 1817 by a Lamar relative, Henry Johnson, who had moved from Maryland to Indiana. The cover page says "To Mr. Robert Johnson, Frederick County Maryland, near middle Town There."

"Dearest Brother," the letter begins,

with the tenderest affection I trouble you with these few

lines whereby I have to inform you that through mercy I am
yet alive and in reasonable health at my age, though I was
badly hurt by a fall off a horse, I lay a long time unable to
turn myself in bed or ever expecting to walk again, but
blessed be the Lord He has raised me again so that I can walk
without limping though I crutched it a long time. If I died
of the hurt it would not been laid to whiskey for I drink
none of the Ruinous Liquid while I live, still I am under no
oath. On the occasion, dear Brother, I received the letter you
sent by Mr. Loveless I considered you was so discomposed
by Reason of the Distress of Sickness your letter was quite
short. Brother when you write again, I wish you would be
more full in accounts, let me know who is alive and who are
deceased of our Relations, and also our old neighbors, also I
would be glad to hear of how is the winter in them parts, it
has been the hardest I ever saw in the western country and
very much the coldest. There has been some complaints of
sickness among us but we are all yet alive that resides in these
parts. Abner Davis and his family is gone away over the
Wabash Rivour I have not heard from them lately. Our kins
people in those parts are all in health or was very lately.
Brother I consider this world a world of Trouble and still we
are not willing to leave it, but wisdom would be to strive to
prepare for death Before it be to late O terrible the consequences to meet death unprepared. Brother read this with
your family. Adam Johnson and Thomas Whiteakor last fall
finally proposed going to Majur Rivour but—They have
Entirely given out moving they find fault with terms of
procuring land the lowest terms is shure not to be under
two dollars per acre and perhaps a great deal higher-some
have moved over into that fine Country with the view of
getting land at 2 dollars per acre and in the Rounds had to
pay ten times that per acre, so we consider best to stay where
we are we are far apart. How glad I would be to be with you
a while but the distance is great and I am old and weakly still

I want to go once more to see you, but I meet with so many disruptions that I don't know when it may or whether it will ever come to pass. I hope you will excuse it as I am sending this letter by a Maryland Gentleman and I can't detain him. I hope you will except of my love to yourself and of family Remember one to all my kin people and my acquaintances includes your affectionate brother.
[signed]

Henry Johnson

The Maryland gentleman who was to carry the letter may not have been quite ready to leave, because Henry found some additional time to write a few more lines. Realizing that it was impossible to return to Maryland, he attempted to entice his brother to move to Indiana.

My family all gives their love to you. My two little grandsons Named after you is uncommon likely little fellows and has very curled hair one is Beckes the other Cateys children near of an age.

Brother there is two hundred acres of land within 4 miles of me I am apprehensive that it might be purchased for about 4000 dollars. There is three plantations on the survey and if it belonged to me I would not take ten thousand and it belongs to three men that wants to be moving. Meditate and write to me mind they are healthy with fine water at Each place with fine orchards on Each place, etc.
[signed]

Henry Johnson

P.S. I have often thought about the Caution you gave me on accounts of the Claim lying near or on Middle Creek I have often guessed how the events would be I would like to hear something about it.

H. Johnson

The early Lamar settlers in the south and west did find the lands they sought, and over time they prospered and multiplied extensively. They were mainly responsible for the spread of the name into South Carolina and Georgia, and then still further toward the ever-expanding frontier. All of the Lamars whose names are today found in history books are descended from these pioneers.

2

LUCIUS QUINTUS CINCINNATUS LAMAR:

Prelude to Secession

Without question, Lucius Quintus Cincinnatus Lamar is the best-known—at least nationally—member of the family.* Not only did he sit on the highest court in the land, but he had earlier been Secretary of the Interior, a Congressman from Mississippi (both before and for many years after the Civil War) , and a United States Senator. In his day he was also widely known and highly respected as a powerful orator. He has been written about more often than any of the other Lamars.

Lucius Quintus Cincinnatus Lamar was born September 17, 1825 outside of Eatonton in Putnam County, Georgia. His grandfather was "Little River" John Lamar, whose plantation property along that river earned him his geographically descriptive nickname. Writing about his grandfather in a letter to his son in 1877, L.Q.C. Lamar, recalled his grandfather's house and 900 acres: "According to my recollection the place is beautiful. A large framed house, an immense front yard full of great oaks and Lombardy poplars, rolling land to the east, and a widespread plain in the rear, shelving gradually down to a beautiful river that gave to the owner of the place (my grandfather) the title 'Little River John.' Here, for many years, in great happiness and moderate prosperity, lived this couple of a century ago".

Lucius shared his unusual name with his father, whose own brothers' interesting and unique names—including Mirabeau

Buonaparte Lamar, Jefferson Jackson Lamar, and Thomas Randolph Lamar—reflected the era's fascination with politics and science. Young Lucius even had a cousin named Lavoisier Legrand Lamar. The story is told that an uncle Zachariah, who had reportedly lived with the L.Q.C.'s grandparents, was an avid reader of history and influential in choosing the children's names based on his most recent reading topic. Others claim that this is probably untrue in that Zachariah's own children had more conventional names. The use of the name Cincinnatus by a Revolutionary War Captain from Georgia named Cincinnatus A.L. Lamar further strains the theory that Zachariah was the source of the unusual names.

Al Capp's famous comic strip "Li'l Abner" had a wonderfully named character called—Jubilation T. Cornpone." That character has always brought to mind the fascinating old names in the Lamar family, and while Lucius Quintus Cincinnatus Lamar's name is one of the first that comes to mind in that regard, it certainly is far from being the only one.

Lucius Lamar's grandfather and grandmother were first cousins—she was Rebecca Lamar. Perhaps as a result of this marriage of close cousins, Lucius' father inherited some weakness or illness along with his brilliance. The father was a very successful legal scholar who had developed a solid reputation and legal practice at a fairly young age. He had been widely recognized for his work in compiling the *Laws of Georgia (Reports) 1810—1820*, which he had done at the request of the state legislature. Later he enlarged and revised *Clayton's Georgia Justice,* a legal reference work of fundamental importance to Georgia lawyers for years after it was published. Suddenly, however, he became ill, and he fell into a deep depression. His work and law practice were seriously affected. Finally, on the Fourth of July, he said good-bye to his family and walked out into the garden. A Chekhovian shot rang out, and family members rushed out to discover that he had taken his own life.

His widow brought up the family and educated them in various Georgia schools. One near Covington was chosen for young Lucius Lamar to attend. As the name implies, the Georgia Confer-

ence Manual Labor School had a farm as part of the property where
the boys learned about plantation work. In his later years, Lucius
recalled his experience there:

> I was a delicate boy, never so athletic as my two brothers,
> and being put to work strengthened and toned up my
> whole system. We all had to work three hours every day at
> the ordinary work of a plantation—plowing, hoeing, cut-
> ting wood, picking cotton, and sowing it, pulling fodder
> and every item and every item of a planters [sic] occupation.
> When we left that school we could do not only the ordinary
> drudgery in the best way, but the most expert could shoe a
> horse, make an axe helve, stock a plow or do any plain bit of
> blacksmithing or carpentry. It was a great training for us all,
> for we became perfectly versed in the details of the work of
> a farm—

Later, the "Manual School" was moved to Oxford, Georgia, and
from there Lucius went on to Emory College. Although he was
not an outstanding student, he did well, especially in the classics,
and was always on the debating team. Lucius graduated from Emory
in 1845 and went into the law office of a relative, A.H. Chappell,
in Macon, Georgia. It was the practice of the day to "read the law"
under an established lawyer instead of going to a law school. After
passing the bar two years later, Lucius moved to Covington, Georgia, to open a law practice. He fell in love with and subsequently
married Virginia Longstreet on July 15, 1847. His father-in-law,
Judge Augustus B. Longstreet was the president of Emory College,
and Lucius must have known her as they were growing up in Oxford.

Over the years L.Q.C. and his father-in-law became especially
close, probably more so than most sons-in-law and fathers-in-law.
Lucius had been a young boy when his father had committed
suicide, and Longstreet had had a son who died at an early age.
These shared losses gave both of them a common bond, as each

man became something of a replacement for the deceased kin of the other.

Following Judge Longstreet's move to become head of the University of Mississippi in 1849, the Lamar family moved there, too. Mississippi in that period was a new and growing area, as attested to by Lucius' letter to A.H. Chappell in which he states that

> this is magnificent country for planters. There are men here who left Newton County poor and in debt eight and ten year ago, who now have a good plantation and fifteen to twenty hands, and are buying more every year . . .
>
> There will be a month or two hence, an election of two additional tutors for this university; and as the duties of one of them will not be so onerous as to draw my attention from my profession, I shall apply for it. My motive for this step is to provide myself with ready money until I get a practice, but more particularly to extricate my mother from some pecuniary embarrassments in which she has become involved, rather by untoward circumstances than by her own mismanagement.

Lucius soon established his legal practice, and was also appointed Adjunct Professor of Mathematics at the University of Mississippi. At the end of two years, however, feeling the pull of his native state, Lucius Lamar moved his family back to Covington, Georgia. In 1852 he opened a law practice there in partnership with his friend Robert G. Harper. The practice quickly flourished, and it didn't take long for Lucius to become involved in politics. His initial foray into political waters was successful, and he was elected to the Georgia legislature.

From the time Lucius gave his opening speech, those who heard him agreed that a powerful orator had emerged. He had a unique gift for public speaking, and he could gain the attention of large gatherings of people with his very manner of speaking. Not only was he witty and able to hold the attention of his audiences, but he was able to speak without notes or memorization. An article written by W. B. Hill in 1893 describes Lucius' maiden speech:

> . . . on a motion to reconsider, Mr. Lamar made his first speech. He was then young, not more than 27, with a handsome face, a full head of dark hair, brilliant eyes, in figure rather below the medium height, handsomely dressed, with fine musical voice. He at once attracted the attention of the House. In a short speech of not more than thirty minutes he captured the whole assembly. I remember how he scathed the motives of those who would thus seek to defeat an election that under the law and constitution had been developed upon the General Assembly.
>
> Such excitement as was produced by that speech I never saw in that body. When he finished no one sought to reply. A vote was taken, and a large majority reconsidered the action of the House of the preceding day and the resolution passed with almost a unanimous vote.
>
> His speech was a remarkable exhibition of the power of the orator and logician, and his appeal to his opponents to step manfully and patriotically forward to discharge their duty was so overwhelming that all party spirit was subdued, even in the breast of the most bitter partisan, and none even ventured a reply.

After his law partner Harper fell ill with tuberculosis and was forced to give up the practice of law, Lucius moved his family to Macon and went into practice there. This move, however, proved to be temporary, and by 1855 the Lamars were back in Mississippi. The reasons were twofold: to be closer to the Longstreet family, and to keep his slaves there profitably employed. Lucius had found it difficult to keep them working in Georgia, so he had already sent them to Mississippi for Judge Longstreet to look after. The Judge could do this, because in addition to being President of the Uni-

versity, he had extensive land holdings. Upon his return to Mississippi, Lucius bought an 1100-acre plantation on the banks of the
Tallahatchee River that they named Solitude. Thus settled, Lucius
set out to practice law again, and to that end, the law firm of
Lamar, Mott and Autrey was established in Holly Springs. Several
very happy years were spent both at the plantation, where his
early training at the manual school was put to practical use, and in
his law partnership.

Politics continued to attract Lucius. In 1857 at a political convention in Oxford, his name came up for state senate. When the
Congressional Nominating Convention was held in Holly Springs,
his name was placed in contention, and after fifteen ballots Lucius
Lamar was selected, but not for state senate. He was chosen instead as the candidate for the United States House of Representatives. Lucius Lamar was elected to the United States Congress, and
on December 1, 1857 joined the 35th Congress. As had happened before, it didn't take long for his fellow Congressmen to
recognize him as a powerful orator, albeit one with a strong states'
rights position. In a letter that he wrote to a Mr. B. Rozell of his
district, Lucius said that he had "never been one of those who run
ahead of the issue, who create evils in order that they may destroy
them. I have preferred always a peaceable settlement of political
questions. But I hold to the old motto 'In peace prepare for war.' I
can see too plainly the clouds that are hanging over us. I can hear
and interpret too well the mutterings of an approaching storm. I
have measured the extent of that danger which we must, sooner or
later, look resistantly in the face."

The question of states' rights, and the whole issue of the right
of individuals to own slaves, was very much in the air. Trouble was
brewing, and because of it Lamar—although he re-elected in
1860—was to become, for now, a one-term congressman.

On April 23, 1860 the Democratic national convention
opened in Charleston, South Carolina, with Lamar as a delegate.
The South was against the candidacy of Stephen Douglas, and
when a pro-Douglas platform was adopted, the Alabama delega-

tion protested the action and withdrew from the convention. Their move was quickly followed by Florida, Texas, Arkansas, Mississippi, Louisiana, South Carolina, and Georgia. This foreshadowed much more serious events to follow, for the South and its political leaders had made their decision. When Lamar went to the capital in Washington in December of 1860 to sit in the 36th Congress, he, along with his fellow Southerners did so not to take their seats in Congress but to resign. Dixie had made up its collective mind to go its own way and secede from the United States.

Returning to Mississippi, L.Q.C. Lamar was elected to attend a state convention on secession, and he was chosen as chairman of a committee to prepare an ordinance providing for Mississippi's withdrawal from the Union. There he authored a document with the somewhat lengthy title of "An ordinance to dissolve the union between the State of Mississippi and other States united with her under the compact entitled The Constitution of the United States of America'." On January 9, 1861 the ordinance that Lucius had penned was voted on and accepted. The die was cast: Mississippi had withdrawn from the Union along with the other states that would form the Confederacy. The Civil War would begin on April 12th, when the shore batteries of Charleston, South Carolina opened fire on Fort Sumter.

3

L.Q.C. LAMAR:

War-time service

Lucius Lamar and his law partner quickly made the shift from being lawyers to being soldiers, and they set about to raise a company of volunteers to prepare for the fight that they knew was inevitable. Lucius soon was named commander of that Mississippi company. He was in Richmond at the time of Jefferson Davis' inauguration, and Hudson Strode, in his book on Davis, tells how Lucius Lamar helped the newly inaugurated Southern leader just after the inauguration ceremony. Colonel Lamar, then 35 years of age, was an intimate friend of the Davis family and had called at their home to pay his respects. The new Confederate President told Lamar about his urgent need for a private secretary, since Captain Josleyn, his current secretary, was resigning to enter the army. Lamar, knowing just the type of person the new President wanted, stated that he knew of the ideal man. Burton Norvelle Harrison, a mathematics teacher and law student at the University of Mississippi, had previously told Lucius that he wished to volunteer, either with Lamar's troop or the highly regarded Washington Artillery in New Orleans. Davis asked about Harrison's background, and was told by Lamar that he had compiled a splendid record at Yale—Phi Beta Kappa, Skull & Bones, editor of the *Yale Literary Magazine*—that he knew Greek and Latin, was a good writer, athletic, good looking, and was possessed with the grace to please. The description seemed complete to Davis, and with his questions satisfactorily answered, he advised Lamar that Harrison was accepted for the job without any need for the new Confederate president to so much as meet him. Lamar immediately telegraphed Harrison, who must have been as shocked as he was pleased to receive the telegraph that read, "You are Private Secretary to the President. Come at once." Apparently the recommendation was sound, and proof that the relationship turned out to meet all expectations was the fact that Harrison continued in the position until the war was over.

Also in Richmond at that time was Mary Chesnut, a true Southern belle who was married to a leading member of the Confederacy. Her father, Stephen Decatur Miller, had been a United States Congressman, governor of South Carolina and later a Senator. Her husband had also been elected to the United States Senate but resigned, as did so many other Southerners, in 1860. Mrs. Chesnut faithfully kept a very detailed and fascinating diary that covered much of what went on in and about her life during the war. She had been in Charleston when the war broke out, and wrote about that night:

> The live long night I toss about-at half past four we hear the booming of the cannon. I start up-dress and rush to my sister's in misery. We go on the house top and see the shells bursting. They say our men are wasting ammunition.
> Mr. Chesnut rode about all night in a little open boat to order our batteries to open. He ordered the first guns fired and he resigned first.
> These long hours the regular sound of the cannon roar-men and women rush in, prayers, imprecations. What scenes. Tonight a force will attempt to land. The 'Harriet Lane' has attempted to get in, been shot, her wheel house ruined and she has put to sea. Proud Carolinians, you must conquer on your own soil. The enemy must not land . . .

Later, Mary Chesnut's husband was transferred to the Confederate capital, Richmond, where she joined him. It is from Mary Chesnut that we are able to hear some of the behind-the-scenes views of and opinions on Lucius Lamar. He was mentioned in Mary Chesnut's diary several times as their paths crossed. Her first mention of him is in June of 1861:

> Mrs. McLane is here. Mrs. Davis always has clever women around her. They gravitate to her. Captain Ingraham came with Colonel Lamar. The latter said he could only stay five minutes; he was obliged to go back at once to his camp. This was a little before 8 o'clock; but at twelve he was still talking to us on that sofa. We taunted him with his fine words to the FFV (first families of Virginia) crowd before the Spotswood. He had said 'Virginia has no grievance, she raises her strong arm to catch the blow aimed at her weaker sisters'. He liked it well, however, that we knew his speech by heart.

Again in June, Mrs. Chesnut reported

> Mr. Lamar, who does not love slavery any more than Sumner does—nor more than I do, laughs at the compliment New England pays us. We want to separate from them, to be rid of Yankees forever, at any price, and they hate us so. Yet they would clasp us, or hook us as Polonius has it, to their bosom with hooks of steel. We are an unwilling bride . . . Mr. Lamar says the young men are light-hearted because there is a fight on hand, but those few who look ahead, the clear heads they see all the risk, the loss of land, limb and life; of home, country and wife, yet as in the days of old, they take it for their country's sake.

The armies soon thereafter encamped on the battlefield. Lamar was in the middle of the fighting and was to fall before long, but not of gunshot wounds. Poor health in the form of what was most likely a stroke knocked him down in June. Lamar's son-in-law Edward Mays described the illness as . . . "something like an apoplexy, accompanied by unconsciousness more or less prolonged, and followed by more or less of paralysis of one side."

Mrs. Chesnut reported that

> Poor Mr. Lamar has been brought from his camp; paralysis, or some sort of stroke. Every woman in the house is ready to rush into the Florence Nightingale business. I think I will wait for a wounded man before I make my first effort as a Sister of Charity. Mr. Lamar sent for me. As everybody went, Mrs. Davis setting the example, so did I. He will not die this time. Will men flatter and make eyes until their eyes close in death? Except that he was in bed, with some learned professor at his bedside, and that his wife has been telegraphed for, he was the same old Lamar of the drawing room
>
> As I was fanning the prostrate Lamar, I repeated Mr. Davis' conversation of the night before. He's all right. The fight had to come. We are men, not women. The quarrel had lasted long enough. We hate each other so the fight had to come. Even Homer's heroes, after they had stormed and scolded enough fought like brave men, long and well. If the athlete Sumner had stood on his manhood and training and struck back when Preston Brooks assailed him, Preston Brooks blow need not have been the opening skirmish of the war. Lamar said Yankees don't fight for the fun of it, they always made it pay or let it alone.

In mentioning Brooks and Sumner, L.Q.C. Lamar was referring to a violent attack that had taken place on the floor of Congress in 1856. Brooks, a vehemently pro-slavery South Carolina Congressman, had assaulted the equally staunch abolitionist Senator Charles Sumner of Massachusetts. Sumner, who was seated after having given a speech, found it impossible to get up to defend himself as

Brooks hit him repeatedly with a cane. Sumner never fully recovered from the beating.

Mrs. Chesnut, on the fifth of July, 1861, wrote

> What a day I have passed—not one moments peace. After breakfast went to Mr. Lamar's room—found Mrs. Davis there. He begged me to stay when she left. I sat down and he began to tell me what she said of me. Until that day he had confined himself to praising my beauty! Heaven save the mark. As if I had any, even when I was young-and Mr. Lamar seemed to think there was something better about me than that . . .
>
> Went to tell Mr. Lamar good-bye. Saw his wife-so grateful to me, and I had done nothing. Sat by him a moment, queer man. Held my hand to his heart for a moment and then covered his eyes-made them light the gas for two professors to see me, poor old me . . .

By mid-July, Mrs. Chesnut reported that Lamar was on crutches, and in October she wrote "Woe to those who began this war, if they were not in bitter earnest. Lamar (L.Q.C. and the cleverest man I know) said in Richmond in one of those long talks of ours. 'Slavery is too heavy for us to carry.' "We agreed to take up Davie Crockett's slogan. My country, may she be right, but my country right or wrong."

With his health somewhat recovered by November, Lamar reported back to Richmond. The incompleteness of his recovery is shown by the fact that one leg was reported to be almost useless. In a letter home to his wife he described his condition: "I hope I am really cured of my sickness. I can manage to get along with a stick, though my leg is quite weak and uncertain in its movements[.] My vertigo comes upon me very rarely, and then in a very modified form . . . The President seems more attached to me than ever. Everybody says that it is well known that he loves me. If we ever have peace, I expect I shall be sent as Minister to The Spain or Sardinia . . . "

By April of 1862, near Yorktown, Lamar's regiment first tasted battle. Confederate General Magruder, with some 16,000 men in his command—including Lamar's Nineteenth Mississippi—faced McClellan's force, which was from three to six times as large. McClellan was slow to start the fight, and the outnumbered Confederates began to withdraw on May 3. When the Union forces followed, a plan of battle was drawn which called for an attack on the pursuing Yankees. The objective for Lamar's regiment was to gain control of a wooded area that Union forces were defending with a fortified fence line. Colonel Mott led one wing of the assault and Lamar the other. Soon after the start of the battle, Mott was fatally shot during a charge, and Lamar took over command. General Wilcox, in his official report stated that "The Nineteenth Mississippi, after the fall of its highly esteemed and brave colonel, was commanded during the remainder of the day by its lieutenant colonel L.Q.C. Lamar. This officer, suddenly called to the command of his regiment, acquitted himself creditably throughout the long and stubbornly contested musketry fight, proving himself in all respects a competent, daring and skillful officer."

Lamar's own view of the battle is found in his report to brigade headquarters:

> At about 8:30 A.M., Col C.H. Mott, then commanding our regiment, was ordered by Gen. Wilcox to make a sortie from the second redoubt, on the right of Fort Magruder, through a field into the forest supposed to be occupied by the enemy in large force . . . Col. Mott placed the right wing of the regiment under my command, and directed me to operate with it according to my own discretion. At the command of our colonel the men advanced with great spirit and steadiness. A destructive fire was at once opened upon us by the enemy. In the first volley, as I was afterwards informed, Col. Mott fell, shot through the body while cheering on his

men. The fight became at once general along our whole line.
The men under my command pressed on to the attack with
the utmost eagerness, and yet with perfect coolness, keeping
our line as unbroken as the nature of the ground would
allow, and firing with deliberation and telling effect. The
enemy, partially protected by the fence behind which they
were posted, contested the ground most stubbornly. The
opposing lines could not have been more than thirty yards
apart, and for a time I expected a hand to hand conflict with
the bayonet; but at last, wavering before the impetuosity
and undaunted resolution of our men, the enemy began to
yield the ground, continuing to fire as they retired . . .

The charge had succeeded, but not without great cost. In addition
to the loss of his law partner, twenty percent of Lamar's regiment
was wiped out.

In the middle of May, L.Q.C. fell sick again, not long after the
battle. He had been inspecting the troops on the reviewing field
when he was suddenly struck by a devastating attack.

Again he was carried off by stretcher and ambulance. This
illness ended L.Q.C.'s brief military career. Unable to carry out
the duties of his command, he resigned his commission in October of 1862. This departure from military service most probably
saved his life. It certainly presented him with a unique and most
interesting opportunity to serve President Davis. The Confederate
government was desperate for diplomatic recognition by foreign
governments. It was hoped that such recognition would help both
to gain financing for the fledgling Confederacy, as well as to aid
her in breaking the Union blockade. It was in support of this effort
that in November 1862, Lucius was appointed Special Commissioner of the Confederate States to the Empire of Russia. Since
travel from the South was greatly impeded by the blockade, he
departed for Mexico on December 1, and arrived in London on
March 1, 1863, with Russia as his final destination. Among the
many friends he made in London was the writer, William Makepeace

Thackeray, whose house became Lamar's London abode. While in London he was soon to learn that British recognition for the Southern cause would be difficult, if not impossible, to obtain. Before leaving London he was able to view, as he reported to his wife in a letter of March 19th "the grandest pageant, I presume, that has appeared in London for many years," that being the marriage of the Prince of Wales. The letter went on to report that "I have been with Mr. Mason [Confederate government representative to England] a good deal. He is very popular here. Mr. Adams [Charles Francis, son of John Quincy Adams], the United States Minister, has complained that he was only treated with civility, while Mr. Mason was treated with cordiality." It was not long before Lamar became aware that the chances for recognition of the Confederate government by the British were somewhere between slim and none. Following his stay in England, Lucius went on to Paris, where he was also a special envoy to the Court of France. There he became acquainted with the land of his ancestors, and met the poet Lamartine who stated that the "—tine" added to the Lamar indicated that he was from a younger branch of the same Lamar family as L.Q.C.'s. While in France, L.Q.C. polished his college French and conducted Southern political business. At the same time, he managed to do some sightseeing, including visiting the cathedral at Chartres. This he found to be most impressive and beautiful, and reported the same in letters home to his wife.

John Slidell was the Confederacy's Paris based envoy to the French. Beckles Wilson, in *John Slidell and the Confederates in Paris*, commented about Lucius that

> Lamar struck Paris as an imposing, even picturesque personality, and in his broad-brimmed hat, tightly buttoned frock coat, and hirsute luxuriance he cut a striking figure on the boulevards. Slidell gave a dinner party in his honor and introduced him to several persons intimate with Russian affairs, and in particular a leading member of the Russian colony in Paris. Lamar told them that he attached great

importance to coming to a friendly arrangement with Russia and so offsetting the overtures Seaward had been making
to the Tsar's government which were founded on a complete misapprehension of Northern designs on Russian
America. The Russians asked about slavery, and when Lamar
stated that this was a domestic issue, he was told that for the
Tsar that was the ONLY ISSUE.

After a short time, it became absolutely clear to Lucius Lamar that
the Southern cause was not being received any more warmly in
France than it was in England. This same truth was also coming to
be understood in the blockaded South. Back at home, the Confederate Senate, unhappy with the treatment Southern envoys were
receiving in Europe, began to consider recalling all European envoys. Those who had been nominated but had not been ratified,
including Lamar, were recalled without ratification. In a letter that
August to his wife he wrote "If nothing prevents, I shall start home
on the first of September . . . If you were here I would remain
much longer, as it is necessary for my health. But I suppose it is
my duty to go home and help the fighting . . . There are many
Confederates here-too many, indeed, of those who ought to be
home fighting . . . If I should be captured by the Federals, don't
be alarmed. They will only place me in confinement, if they do
that . . ." With no official reason to remain in Europe, Lucius started
home.

The return trip was very eventful, since the Union blockade of
Southern ports forced him to take a circuitous route. From Europe
he had to sail first to Halifax, then to Bermuda on a British ship.
In Bermuda he secured passage on a blockade runner, the vessel
Ceres. Also aboard was his cousin Charles A.L. Lamar, son of Gazaway
B. Lamar, and former owner of the slave blockade runner *Wan-
derer*. His Lamar cousin had been in Europe during the summer of
1863 arranging to buy ships for the Importing and Exporting
Company of Georgia, founded and controlled by Gazaway Lamar
to run the Union blockade. The plan for *Ceres* was to make the

popular run into the important blockade running port of Wilmington, North Carolina. On the way, she was spotted and chased by a Union patrol. Unable to reach the protection of Confederate forts at the harbor's mouth, the captain ran the *Ceres* aground to save her from capture or sinking. The passengers and crew were forced to take to the boats to save their lives. Lucius Lamar lost almost all his personal belongings, including whatever he was bringing home to his family from Europe; the small amount of luggage he recovered was thoroughly waterlogged. The wife of his good friend Clement Clay noted with a bit of wry humor that Lamar returned "as did many of our returned foreign emissaries, on top of a friendly wave."

Not long after his return to Dixie, Lucius showed up in the Confederate capital, and his activities were again noted in Mary Chesnut's diary. She reported that Lamar was at President Davis' in January of 1864. "At the President's, [Chestnut's husband] saw L.Q.C. Lamar. Unconfirmed by the Senate, he has had to come home from Russia. They must have refused his confirmation simply to anger Jeff Davis. Everybody knows there is not a cleverer man this side of the water than Mr. Lamar or a truer patriot. Lamar is changed so much that at first Mr. Chesnut did not recognize him."

Later that month Lamar was invited to dinner at the Chesnut home, but somehow a mistake was made as to which day the invitation was for.

> Lamar was asked to dinner here yesterday—so he came to-day. We had our wild turkey cooked for him yesterday, and I dressed myself within an inch of my life, with the best of my four year old finery. Two of us, Mr. Chesnut and I, did not damage the wild turkey seriously, and today Lamar enjoyed the rechauffe and he commented on the art with which Molly hid the slight loss we had inflicted upon its mighty breast. She piled fried oysters over the turkey so

skillfully that unless we had told it, no one would have ever known the huge bird was making his second appearance upon the table.

Lamar was more absent minded and distrait than ever, but my husband behaved like a trump, a well-bred man with all his wits about him: so things went off smoothly enough. Lamar had just read Romola. Across the water, he said, it was the rage. I am sure it was not as good as Adam Bede or Silas Marner. It is not worthy of the woman who was to rival all but Shakespeare's name below. What is the matter with Romola? he protested . . . Lamar told us about this writer who so well imagines female purity and piety. She was a governess, or something of that sort, perhaps she wrote for a livelihood. At any rate, she had an "elective affinity," to which he responded, to Lewes; so she lives with Lewes! [Lamar was describing the female author, George Eliot] Lamar does not know whether she caused the separation between Lewes and his legal wife, but he says they were living in a villa on some Swiss lake. She is the Mrs. Lewes of the hour; a charitable, estimable, agreeable, sympathetic woman of genius; a fallen woman, living in a contented, nay a happy state of immorality!

Lamar seemed without prejudice on the subject. At least he expressed neither surprise nor disapprobation. He said something of genius being above law, but I was not very clear as to what he said at that point. As for me, I said nothing, for fear of saying too much. 'My idol was shattered—my day star fled.'

Lewes is a writer. Some people say the man she lives with is a noble man. They say she is kind and good, even if she is a fallen woman. Here the conversation ended.

Again, in February of 1864 Mary Chesnut mentions Lamar, and the comment possibly indicates that a wartime romance or romances had been either contemplated or consummated. "The party for Johnny was the nicest I have ever had, and I mean it to be my last. I sent word to the Cary's to bring their own men. They came alone, saying they did not care for men! "That means a raid on ours" growled Isabelle. Mr. Lamar was devoted to Constance Cary. He is a freelance, so that created no heartburning."*

Still not in the best of health, Lucius Quintus Cincinnatus Lamar did what he could in support of the Confederate cause and of Jefferson Davis, who was coming under increasing political pressure. Lamar traveled to Georgia to speak out against the opposition to Davis, and then to Richmond, where in December 1864 he was commissioned Judge Advocate of the military court of the Third Army Corps. By now, both his law partners and both his brothers, as well as many other friends and relatives, had perished on the battlefield. His younger brother, Jefferson Mirabeau Lamar, had died while serving under Howell Cobb at the battle for Crampton's Gap in Maryland, a bloody skirmish that was a prelude to Antietam. His other brother, Thompson Bird Lamar, Colonel of the Fifth Florida, had survived severe wounds at Antietam, only to be killed at Petersburg. Knowledge of these deaths did not appear to instill in Lamar any fear of exposure to enemy fire. When L.Q.C. was asked to address some of the Mississippi troops then stationed in Virginia, reports indicate that Lamar spoke to them while standing on a stump, in sight and range of enemy rifles. Given as he was to public speaking, he gave a highly motivating speech, but at great risk to his own life. He was ultimately pulled down from the splintered stump from which he was speaking only after one too many enemy bullets had passed so dangerously close to him that his audience wouldn't allow him to continue to take the risk any longer. General Harris, whose troops Lucius had addressed, described the scene as follows: "Never shall I forget that scene: the earnest faces and torn and tattered uniforms of officers and men as shown by the flickering torchlights, the rattle of the musketry on the skirmish line, the heavy detonation of the enemy's constant artillery fire, the eloquent and burning words of the speaker, and the wild cheers of the auditors, stirred to the innermost depths of their hearts by his patriotic words." Lamar concluded his speech by declaring "Those Yankees must have owl's eyes."

Unlike the optimistic and bellicose opening days of the war, the Southern troops were plainly tired, their ranks painfully thinned, and the end of the war was only a matter of time. The military might of the Union and the blockade of Confederate ports had succeeded in choking the South's commerce and military logistics, bringing on a slow and agonizing death. The critical ports of Charleston and Wilmington were choked and finally closed down altogether by the Federal blockade.

Finally, in April of 1865 Robert E. Lee's Army of Northern Virginia was ordered to fight no more, and the weary soldiers of the Confederacy began their long march home from Appomattox Court House.

4

L.Q.C. LAMAR:

Rebuilding from the Ashes

On May 20, 1865, with his duties as Judge Advocate finally completed, Lucius Quintus Cincinnatus Lamar started home from Richmond to his family in Mississippi. On this trek he was accompanied by General E.C. Walthall, a Virginia native who had grown up in Mississippi. The two had great respect for each other, and eventually Lamar joined Walthall in a law partnership in Coffeeville, Mississippi.* A letter written by Mrs. Lamar to her mother Mrs. Longstreet in February of 1866 tells us something of these hard, bitter times: "Perhaps it will turn out right in the end. I try to take this view of everything which happens, and be thankful for the portion of this world's goods which is left to us. True, the times are very much changed, but they might be worse. We keep no man servant now about the lot. Lucius has been working about the fences and gates and locks to the outhouses. He feeds his cows and helps cut the wood and does a great deal of work. If he can only have good health, I feel as if we would be happy under almost any circumstances."

A stark reminder of just how much the times had changed was brought to the family's attention in the form of a sign from his pre-war law firm of Lamar, Mott and Autrey. It had been ripped from its post by the Union forces and thrown into the river, and it had later been recovered, battered and broken, floating toward the Gulf of Mexico. Finding that sad artifact of happier, prosperous days when his two law partners (and brothers) were still alive had to be a very bitter reminder of just how bad the times were, and how much had been lost in the bloody conflict.

By June of 1866 Lamar had been asked to resume his professorship at the University of Mississippi. Since this position also allowed him to also practice law, he accepted and soon moved his family back to Oxford.

Several of the young men in Lamar's wartime regiment had, at the start of the war, left various colleges to join the armed forces of the Confederacy. Some of them, upon hearing that Lamar was to be a professor at the University of Mississippi, chose to study under their former leader. One of those student-soldiers, although not of Lamar's regiment, Thomas B. Manlove, had been a member of the Sigma Alpha Epsilon fraternity at the old University of Nashville. When he, along with a group of Lamar's ex-soldiers, set about to form a Sigma Alpha Epsilon chapter at Ole Miss, they naturally invited their celebrated professor to join them. He accepted and was initiated into the fraternity along with them, in spite of the fact that many years had passed since he had been an undergraduate.

The war had left the Lamar property in ruins and its finances in debt. In order to help put their finances in order, the family sold off many treasured heirlooms, including the silverware. A small mortgage that had been well within L.Q.C.'s income before the war now became a millstone around his neck that was paid off only after a long period of time and with great difficulty and sacrifice. Times were indeed very hard financially, and even harder politically. As can be imagined, the post-war "carpetbagger" years were not only extremely difficult for the residents of the occupied South, but the actions of the occupation troops and the carpetbag government bordered on, or crossed the line into, lawlessness. In writing to the then imprisoned Jefferson Davis, Lucius described these bleak times: "Spies and secret detectives swarm through the country, dogging the footsteps of our best citizens, following up with arrests, arbitrary searches, indefinite and unexplained imprisonments, trials before vindictive and partisan juries for the purpose of insuring convictions."

Lamar realized and believed that the best possibility for relief of the Southern people was to not continue the old arguments that had led to the war, but to restore normal state functions and remove the military occupation forces. He worked at this for several years, making little progress at first. In time, however, his persistence would pay off.

L.Q.C. Lamar's private life went through profound changes in the span of eight months in 1868 and 1869. In November of 1868, his mother-in-law passed away. In May his daughter was married to Mr. Edward Mayes, who was later to be Chancellor of the University of Mississippi. Two months later, L.Q.C.'s beloved father-in-law passed away. Because of the closeness of the two men, this must have been another very difficult period of time.

The carpetbag suppression of the South finally began to ease after some of the excesses became more widely known, and public pressure was brought to bear that resulted in bringing the lawlessness of early Reconstruction under control.

5

L.Q.C. LAMAR:

From Senator to Supreme Court Justice

On February 23, 1870, Mississippi was readmitted to the Union, and by August 1872, L.Q.C. Lamar had been nominated for the U. S. Congress. Despite the fact that he was barred from holding that office due to his prior activities in support of the Confederacy, he won the election. In December of 1872, Lucius Lamar went to Washington where he presented a petition that, if allowed, would permit him to occupy the seat that he had won. The House of Representatives voted 111 in favor and 13 against. Later the Senate voted unanimously in favor of the petition, leaving Lamar free to take his seat. The outcome of this vote probably reflects on both the personal likability of L.Q.C. (who spent a good deal of time in Washington visiting those who might help his cause), as well as the knowledge that he was a pragmatic Southerner ready to help with the healing process. In December of 1873 he joined the 43rd Congress and immediately sought out an opportunity to make a speech that would be heard widely and that would nurture the healing process. The "bloody shirt" was often dragged out and waved by politicians seeking to keep the South in a position of subjugation.

Others in the Congress had previously attempted to convey the message that it was time to start the healing process, but their words had fallen on deaf ears. Perhaps they were too early or lacked the speaking power or the reputation, but for whatever reason no

others had successfully gotten the message across to the general
public or to the Congress. Commenting on the time leading up to
his speech on that subject, Lamar wrote to Alabaman Clement
Clay, a longtime friend, that what "was wanted was an occasion on
which they would listen & listen with something of a feeling of
sympathy. I thought on the death of Sumner was such an occasion." Charles Sumner was the same Senator from Massachusetts
who had before the war been beaten on the Senate floor by Preston
Brooks. He had long been an outspoken abolitionist who after the
war had advocated an amnesty for former Confederates. L.Q.C.
was invited, or wangled himself an invitation, to give a eulogy to
Congress.

Lamar's speech was a short and pointed. After extolling
Sumner's character, intellect, and dedication to the freedom of
slaves, he spoke of Sumner's post-war sympathy for the population
of the fallen South:

> Mr. Speaker—In rising to second the resolutions just of-
> fered, I desire to add a few remarks which have occurred to
> me as appropriate to the occasion. I believe that they express
> a sentiment which pervades the hearts of all the people
> whose representatives are here assembled. Strange as, in look-
> ing back upon the past, the assertion may seem, impossible
> as it would have been ten years ago to make it, it is not the
> less true that today Mississippi regrets the death of Charles
> Sumner, and sincerely unites in paying honor to his
> memory . . . It has been the kindness of the sympathy which
> in these later years he has displayed toward the impover-
> ished and suffering people of the Southern States that has
> unveiled to me the generous and tender heart which beat
> beneath the bosom of the zealot, and has forced me to yield
> him the tribute of my respect—I might even say of my
> admiration . . .
> Charles Sumner in life believed that all occasion for strife
> and distrust between the North and South had passed away,

and there no longer remained any cause for continued estrangement between these two sections of our common country. Are there not many of us who believe the same thing? . . . Shall we not, over the honored remains of this great champion of human liberty, this feeling sympathizer with human sorrow, this earnest pleader for the exercise of human tenderness and charity, lay aside the concealments which serve only to perpetuate misunderstandings and distrust, and frankly confess that on both sides we most earnestly desire to be one . . .

Would that the spirit of the illustrious dead whom we lament today could speak from the grave to both parties to this deplorable discord in tones which should reach each and every heart throughout this broad territory: My countrymen! know one another and you will love one another.

Lamar's own pleasure with the speech can be seen in a letter that he wrote to his wife the following day:

I never in all my life opened my lips with a purpose more single to the interests of our Southern people than when I made this speech. I wanted to seize an opportunity when universal attention could be arrested, and directed to what I was saying, to speak to the North in behalf of my own people. I succeeded fully, but not more fully than I anticipated. I will send you letters which will show you what a tremendous revolution of feeling it has wrought in Boston and New York toward the South. I did not aim at rhetorical or personal success, so earnest and engrossing was my other object, but the rhetorical triumph was as prodigious as it was unexpected . . . One of the most gratifying features of the occasion was that my son was in the gallery, and witnessed the greatest triumph his father has ever won.

This very powerful and moving speech, like almost all that Lamar gave, was delivered without help of notes or written text. L.Q.C. believed that prepared speeches constrained and limited him. Writing to a cousin, Mrs. John C. Butler, of Macon, Georgia, Lamar said " . . . I cannot write a speech. The pen is an extinguisher upon my mind and a torture to my nerves. I am the most habitual ex-temporaneous speaker that I have ever known. . . . But my friends tell me that my off hand speeches are by far more vivid than my prepared efforts."

The *New York Tribune* on April 28, 1874 reported of Lamar's speech that a " . . . spontaneous burst of applause went up from Republicans and Democrats alike." The North was by now start-ing to realize that the post-war treatment of the South which had inflicted extreme suffering on the residents of those states was not appropriate. The politicians of the North were now willing to lis-ten to one of the native son's of the South, especially one of the well educated "planter" class who had long been among the South's political leaders, call in a most eloquent way for the healing to begin. The *Springfield (Mass.) Republican* reported: "When such a Southerner of the Southerners as Mr. Lamar of Mississippi, stands up in the House of Representatives to pronounce such a generous and tender eulogy upon Charles Sumner as this which the (tele-graph) wires bring us this morning, it must begin to dawn upon the most inveterate rebel haters in Congress, and the press, that the war is indeed over, and that universal amnesty is in order." There were also signs in the South that such a call could be made without causing immediate political suicide. A month before Lamar's speech, Democrats and Republicans in the Mississippi legislature had joined in paying tribute to the fallen Sumner.

In March of 1875 Lamar was invited to help campaign for Democratic candidates and took the occasion to make a speech in Nashua, New Hampshire. "I have come under the persuasion that the citizens of this state, as indeed the people all over the country, desire that the era of sectional discord and alienation and strife from which the country has been so long suffering shall be brought to a close, and that a new one shall be inaugurated which shall be

illustrious as an era of cordial reunion between the sections . . ."
L.Q.C. Lamar attempted to put to rest Yankee concerns and to
assure his audience that the return of local self-government in the
South would not put at risk personal liberty and political rights
for Americans of all classes and races, especially including the recently emancipated former slaves. He told them that the South
accepted the new amendments to the Constitution, and told them
that the recent disorders in his region were due to federal interfer-
ence which had forced honest and intelligent people out of public
office. Details of official corruption uncovered by Congressional
investigations were presented, and Lamar went on to conclude: "If
you were to attempt to confer a separate nationality upon them,
they [Southerners] would not accept it as a boon. They all believe,
and feel in their shattered condition, that their hope and the hope
of the American people is the preservation of the Union . . . Just
vouchsafe to them the benefits of government as you enjoy them
yourselves. Give them the right of local self government, that is all
they ask, and they will teach their children to lisp 'Liberty and
Union, now and forever, one and inseparable."

The reaction of the Northern press is reflected in the article in
the *Boston Advertiser* dated March 7, 1875:

> Lamar of Mississippi, spoke to the citizens of Nashua last
> evening on the condition of his people at the South. Though
> the hall was engaged by the Democratic Committee, and he
> was invited to speak, it was by no means a party gathering
> that assembled. Republicans and Democrats, attracted by
> the reputation which he bears for eloquence, ability and
> worth crowded the large hall till they filled it to overflow-
> ing. His address was exactly suited to the mixed character of
> his audience. It was remarkably non-partisan, consisting
> merely of a statement of facts braced by the reports of Con-
> gressional investigations and a logical tracing of the causes
> which have led to whatever turbulence and disquietude
> exist; containing scarcely an allusion to either of the two

> political parties, and none whatever to the approaching election. He spoke for about two hours, not concluding till nearly eleven o' clock, and retained the closest attention to the last; and then, as several times before, there were loud calls for him to continue . . .

In spite of the approbation of the Northern press, Lamar's correspondence of the period indicates that the Sumner speech did cause concern among some of his friends and fellow politicians who were not in complete agreement with all that he said of Sumner. But any reservations that they had were momentary and had little long-term effect. When he ran for reelection, Lamar actively led his party in seeking to oust the corrupt carpetbag state government. At a party meeting in 1875, Lamar wrote up a list of grievances that showed some of the suffering caused by five years of carpetbag government: taxes had risen fourteen-fold, and four-fifths of the town of Greenville had been put up for tax auction sale. The carpetbag Governor Ames (from Maine), who had been military Governor and then had won a questionable public election, knew that he was in trouble at the polls. Fearing impending defeat if he could not control the ballot boxes, Ames implored President Grant to again send in Federal troops. Ames sent the President a telegram saying "Domestic violence, in its most aggravated form, exists in certain parts of this State." Grant refused his request due to the increasing public pressure brought on, in no small part, by Lamar and his speeches.

The Democrats waged a hard campaign, won the election, and returned Lamar to Congress. In their battle to win back the governorship of the state, they had articles of impeachment filed against Governor Ames. Ames, realizing he was trapped, agreed to resign if and when the charges were dropped. Charges were quickly dropped, and he did resign. The Superintendent of Education, T. W. Cordozo had resigned rather than face trial, and Lieutenant Governor Davis, was convicted of bribery and removed from office.

During Lamar's second term in Congress the Democratic party

made plans to select a candidate for Senate, as the term of Mississippi Senator James L. Alcorn was due to expire in March of 1877. At the Democratic-Conservative caucus several names including Lamar's were in contention, but all others were withdrawn prior to balloting and Lamar was voted by acclaim in a single ballot without any dissenters. On January 19th the Mississippi Legislature elected him Senator by an almost unanimous vote of both Houses. Lucius Lamar's statesmanship in promoting the healing process between the North and South had been recognized and rewarded.

Lamar's entry to the upper house came at the same time that the great silver debate was coming to a boil. During the early 1870s, Congress had voted to keep silver coins from being legal tender for amounts greater than five dollars. This, in effect, put the United States on the gold standard. New silver mines in the West had vastly increased the supply of that precious metal, thereby causing its value to drop substantially, especially when compared to gold. 1873 was a year of economic panic, and in that time of financial depression those who owed money were attracted to any means of paying off debt with "cheaper" dollars. "Silver Dick" Bland of Missouri had introduced a bill calling for the free coinage of silver, and easy money was an appealing concept to many, and most especially to the impoverished voters of Mississippi.

After extensive study of the subject, Lamar concluded that utilizing cheap silver dollars, worth perhaps 10% less than the face value of the original debt, to pay back obligations was not the right thing for the country to do. On January 24, 1878 he made his first major speech in the Senate, one in which he went against the wishes of the Mississippi electorate and laid out his belief that while many people hoped for economic relief through free silver coinage, he didn't believe that the switch to silver would have that result. He saw that while payment of bonds with debased silver would offer immediate savings, refinance of the debt would be at a more expensive, perhaps prohibitive rate to make up for earlier as well as potential future loss. The state legislature in Mississippi had already passed a resolution instructing the state's senators to vote in favor of the Bland Bill. The final vote in Congress was delayed until mid-February, and on the 15th of that month Lamar rose to speak a second time. "Mr. President, having already expressed my deliberate opinion at some length upon this very important measure now under consideration, I shall not trespass upon the attention of the Senate further. I have, however, one other duty to perform; a very painful one, I admit, but one which is nonetheless clear. I hold in my hand certain resolutions of the Legislature of Mississippi which I have to read." The clerk then read the resolutions requiring Mississippi's senators to vote yes vote on the matter, and Lamar concluded his remarks with a powerful voice that "grew tremulous with emotion":

> Mr. President: Between these resolutions and my convictions there is a great gulf. I cannot pass it. Of my love to the State of Mississippi I will not speak; my life alone can tell it. My gratitude for all the honor her people have done me, no words can express. I am best proving it by doing day to day what I think their true interests and their character require me to do. During my life in that State, it has been my privilege to assist in the education of more than one generation of her youth, to have given the impulse to wave after wave of the young manhood that has passed into the troubled seas of her social and political life. Upon them I have always endeavored to impress the belief that truth was better than falsehood, honesty better than policy, courage better than cowardice. Today my lessons confront me. Today I must be true or false, honest or cunning, faithful or unfaithful to my people. Even in this hour of their legislative displeasure and disapprobation I cannot vote these resolutions direct. I cannot and will not shirk the responsibility which my position imposes. My duty, as I see it, I will do; and I will vote against this bill. When that is done my responsibility is ended. My reasons for my vote shall be given to my people. Then it will

be for them to determine if adherence to my honest convictions has disqualified me from representing them; whether a
difference of opinion upon a difficult and complicated subject to which I have given patient, long continued, consci-
entious study, to which I have brought entire honesty and
singleness of purpose, and upon which I have spent whatever ability God has given me, is now to separate us; whether
this difference is to override that complete union of thought,
sympathy, and hope which on all other and, as I believe,
even more important subjects, binds us together. Before
them I must stand or fall; but be their present decision what
it may, I know that the time is not far distant when they will
recognize my action today as wise and just; and, armed with
honest convictions of my duty, I shall calmly await results
believing in the utterances of a great American who never
trusted his country in vain, that 'truth is omnipotent, and
public justice certain.'

Lamar's stand against the bill and his defiance of the will of the
Mississippi Legislature were in spite of the fact that the bill had
enough support in the Senate to not only get passed, but also to
overcome a veto by President Hayes. Thus, Lamar's opposition to
the bill was completely a matter of principle; his vote against the
bill had no chance of helping to stop the bill's passage.

While those who stood against the bill praised Lamar, the general sentiment, especially in his home state, was that he was to
going to be a one-term Senator. Realizing this, Lamar took his
message to the people of Mississippi, repeatedly touring the state
to talk to thousands of voters. He let them know that he realized
that his stand had not pleased them, and he went onto explain his
position by describing Constitutional history and giving examples
of other famous Senators who had found cause to go against legislative orders. He also told a parable of an incident that he said had
happened during the war, and although he didn't name the ship,
it was possibly influenced by his experience aboard the blockade

runner *Ceres.* The story was about a blockade runner during the Civil War, bound for Savannah harbor. The Captain asked his senior officers if the Union gunboats could be in the harbor. They thought they knew where the enemy was and strongly proclaimed that the enemy boats were not in Savannah. The Captain then sent a young sailor, Billy Summers, atop the mast with a telescope. From that lofty perch, Billy was able to identify masts in the river belonging to the enemy boats. His warning saved the blockade runner, along with its crew and passengers, from capture. The Captain was willing to override the advice of his senior officers because Billy, just a sailor, had the best opportunity to see what was out of sight to those on deck. Lamar told the people that he was not wiser than the Mississippi legislature, but as a member of the United States Senate he was in a better position to see what was in the best interests of the people of Mississippi, just as Billy Summers had been in a better position to see danger than the ship's officers were.

> Thus it is, my countrymen, you have sent me to the topmost mast, and I tell you what I see. If you say I must come down, I will obey without a murmur, for you can not make me lie to you; but if you return me, I can only say that I will always be true . . . I have always thought that the first duty of a public man in a Republic founded upon the sovereignty of the people is a frank and sincere expression of his opinions to his constituents. I prize the confidence of the people of Mississippi, but I never made popularity the standard of my action. I profoundly respect public opinion, but I believe that there is a conscious rectitude of purpose, a sustaining power which will support a man of ordinary firmness under any circumstances whatever.

As this trip through Mississippi continued, evidence grew to indicate that Lamar's message was being heard. The attitude of those entering the meetings was vastly different from those leaving the same meetings a few hours later. Jeers changed to cheers, and the prospect of Lamar becoming a one-term Senator soon faded. One sign of the affection those who lived around his home base at the University of Mississippi held for him was seen upon his return to the University after the end of the Congressional session in 1878. When he entered the chapel for graduation ceremonies, his first public appearance there since returning from Washington, the crowd gave him a standing ovation that lasted several minutes.

In 1882 he won the election and was returned to the Senate. The story about old Billy Summers and L.Q.C.'s persuasive way of delivering it was probably a lot more to thank for the positive outcome of that campaign than any number of explanations of monetary policy. It was, in part, because of this unpopular stand that John F. Kennedy included L.Q.C. Lamar in *Profiles in Courage.*

Lamar had remained a loyal personal supporter of his old friend and leader Jefferson Davis. When a resolution came before the Senate concerning pensions for soldiers of the War of 1812, Senator Hoar of Massachusetts proposed an amendment as follows: "Provided further, That no pension shall ever be paid under this act to Jefferson Davis, the late President of the so called Confederacy." A great debate followed, from which Lamar remained aloof until Hoar, in answer to Senator Garland said "the Senator from Arkansas alluded to the courage which this gentleman had shown in battle, and I do not deny it. Two of the bravest officers of our Revolutionary War were Aaron Burr and Benedict Arnold." Lamar was greatly angered to hear Davis equated to the traitors Burr and Arnold and rose to speak. He was declared out of order until the chair finally allowed him to take the floor. "Now, Mr. President, having been decided by my associates to have been in order, in the language I used, I desire to say that, if it is at all offensive or unacceptable to any member of this Senate, the language is withdrawn; for that is not my purpose to offend or stab the sensibilities of any of my associates on this floor. But what I meant by that remark was this: Jefferson Davis stands in precisely the position that I stand in, that every Southern man who believed in the right of a state to secede stands." Hoar then spoke, saying that he did not mean to bar Lamar from the pension, and Lamar continued

> The only difference between myself and Jefferson Davis is that his exalted character, his preeminent talents, his well established reputation as a statesman, as a patriot, and as a soldier, enabled him to take the lead in the cause to which I consecrated myself and to which every fiber of my heart responded. There was no distinction between insult to him and the Southern people, except that he was their chosen leader, and they his enthusiastic followers; and there has been no difference since.
>
> Jefferson Davis, since the war, has never counseled insurrection against the authority of this government. Not one word has he uttered inconsistent with the greatness and glory of this American Republic. The Senator from Massachusetts can point to no utterance of Jefferson Davis which bids the people of the South to cherish animosities and hostilities to this Union, nor does he cherish them himself.
>
> The Senator—it pains me to say it—not only introduced this amendment, but he coupled that honored name with treason; for, sir, he is honored among the Southern people. He did only what they sought to do; he was simply chosen to lead them in a cause which we all cherished; and his name will continue to be honored for his participation in that great movement which inspired an entire people, the people who were animated by motives as sacred and noble as ever inspired the breast of a Hamden or a Washington. I say this as a Union man today. The people of the South drank their inspiration from the fountain of devotion to liberty and to constitutional government. We believed that we were fighting for it, and the Senator cannot put his finger upon one distinction between the people of the South and the man whom the Senator has today selected for dishonor as the representative of the South.

> Now, sir, I do not wish to make any remarks here that will
> engender any excitement or discussion; but I say that the
> Senator from Massachusetts connected that name with trea-
> son. We all know that the results of this war have attached to
> the people of the South the technical crime of rebellion, and
> we submit to it; but that was not the sense in which the
> gentleman used that term as applied to Mr. Davis. He in-
> tended to affix (I will not say that he intended, but the
> inevitable effect of it was to affix) upon this aged man, this
> man broken in fortune, suffering from bereavement, an
> epithet of odium, an imputation of moral turpitude.
> Sir, it required no courage to do that; it required no magna-
> nimity to do it; it required no courtesy. It only required hate,
> bitter, malignant, sectional feeling, and a sense of personal
> impunity. The gentleman, I believe, takes rank among Chris-
> tian statesmen. He might have learned a better lesson even
> from the pages of mythology. When Prometheus was bound
> to the rock, it was not an eagle, it was a vulture, that buried
> his beak in the tortured vitals of the victim.

While nearing the end of his speech, Lamar held his arms high
and, while pronouncing the word eagle, carved the outline of an
eagle in the air. The hand flowingly changed from sculpting the
eagle, and pointed directly at Hoar as Lamar hissed out "it was a
vulture." Lamar had dramatically and graphically made his point.
Hoar backed off. In spite of crossing swords on the Senate floor,
Hoar and Lucius continued to hold each other in high regard.

The Presidential campaign of 1884 saw Grover Cleveland as
the Democratic nominee, and Lamar backed the party candidate
through active campaigning. The South went strongly for Cleveland, giving him 107 of his total votes in the electoral college.
With the repressive Republicans out of leadership, the South,
through her former and heretofore tainted leaders, could now be
included in the top echelons of government. Lamar was chosen by

Cleveland as Secretary of the Interior in spite of Lamar's protests that he could be of greater help in the Senate.

At about that time, Lucius was looking for a house to rent in Washington. Upon hearing that Mrs. Dahlgren, the widow of the Admiral, had recently constructed a luxurious house, he went to see her about renting it. After viewing it, Lucius asked how much rent she wanted and the reply came, $7500 a year. For a long time Lucius said nothing; finally the widow Dahlgren asked if he was sick. No, he replied, I was just thinking about what I would do with the remainder of my salary. Some of his friends heard the story, and found it amusing enough to record for posterity, since it was well known that his salary as a cabinet member was but $8,000 a year.

Another story about Lucius related to his reading habits, since he was known to read a wide range of many sorts of books, mostly of a serious nature and including many classics. One day while on his way into the White House, Lucius tripped and dropped his brief case, out of which fell several books. The reporters who were gathered about helped him pick them up and put them back in his case. They were amused to discover that the Secretary's reading was not dry government statistics or the classics as might have been expected, but light novels.

The Interior Department had responsibility for two activities which were large problem areas since they were highly subject to fraud; the Land Office and Pension Bureau. The United States government owned vast amounts of open land and had responsibility for Indian lands. Both of these were being invaded by illegal settlers as well as railroads and cattle barons who fenced off vast areas of public or Indian land without proper, or in some cases any, compensation. In the other problem area, pension expenditures under Lamar's predecessor had shot up from $5 million to $30 million a year in less than three years. These problem areas were attacked with the straight forward logic and problem-solving that he had exhibited in other areas of endeavor. At the same time the relationship between the President and his Secretary grew from one of advisor into one of friend. L.Q. C. produced annual reports about his Department that detailed areas that needed attention as well as areas of positive accomplishment. At the time of the third annual report, the accomplishments were substantial, in many cases because of Lamar's ability to work with Congress to obtain legislation necessary to correct problems. One of the more meaningful accomplishments that he helped achieve was the establishment of the Interstate Commerce Commission to regulate railroad tariffs. Prior to the passage of that legislation the antics of the "Robber Barons" of the railroad industry were legendary. One measure of Lamar's national reputation was the number of honorary degrees that he received. One of those was from Harvard University, given in 1886 at the 250th anniversary of the founding of that solidly Yankee institution. There, this former Confederate was awarded a Doctorate of Laws.

In spite of his generally favorable national reputation, when Cleveland submitted his nomination to the Supreme Court in December, 1887, Lamar's Republican opponents and enemies in Congress thought their time had come to cause him trouble. In January the Judiciary Committee of the Senate presented their majority opinion against Lamar's appointment, claiming that the nominee was both too old and too many years removed from the practice of law. Voting had been along party lines and the outcome of the full vote seemed bleak, since there were 38 Republicans, 37 Democrats, and one Independent. Three months earlier the nomination probably would have passed easily, but political pressures had increased. Political expediency appeared to dictate defeat, or at least that's what the Republican opposition hoped. The outcome was unclear, and the chances of success were small. Both sides worked the corridors and smoke-filled rooms to sway the majority to their persuasion and Lamar put his ability to speak extemporaneously to good use. When the vote was finally taken on January 16th, Lamar the underdog had carried the day. The votes were 32 for Lamar and 28 against. Because the Republicans had failed to vote as a block, 16 had abstained; Lamar's appointment was won.

The first several years that L.Q.C. was on the bench were productive, and the opinions that he wrote were generally looked upon favorably. His logical mind produced clearly thought-out opinions that were well received by lawyers, by fellow justices, and by the President. He generally was in agreement with the majority and seldom dissented. Perhaps this reflected his ability to communicate his ideas to others and win over his fellow justices in discussions. Possibly his years of reconciling North and South had influenced his thinking, so that he sought to agree with his fellow justices rather than differ.

Age was creeping up on the professor-legislator-warrior-diplomat-senator-cabinet member-jurist. The illness that had afflicted him from time-to-time throughout his life was reappeared in 1892. This time its effects were permanent. Although he was able to carry on his court duties for a time, just prior to Christmas of that year he and his wife departed Washington and took a train trip to the Mississippi coast for his health. During the trip he took a turn for the worse, so bad that he had to be taken from the train in Atlanta. It turned out that he had suffered a heart attack. Several days later he went on to Macon in his native Georgia, where on January 23, 1893 he felt well enough to take the trolley into downtown Macon. There he ran into "Doc" Flewellen, a college friend from Emory, and they enjoyed the afternoon. Later he invited "Doc" to have dinner with his family. Soon after "Doc" left, a final and fatal stroke brought this most productive and interesting life to end.

Lamar's burial was in his native Georgia and was reported in the *Memphis Commercial-Appeal* on October 26, 1894: "There was laid to rest to-day in the beautiful St. Peter's Cemetery, among a solid bank of flowers, all that was mortal of the late Justice L.Q.C. Lamar, the South's greatest orator and statesman."

6

GAZAWAY BUGG LAMAR:

Financier and Steamboat Pioneer

What a name! Bugg was the maiden name of the first two of his grandfather's wives. The Gazaway name derived from the Gassaways of Colonial Maryland and had been used by Lamar ancestors. Basil Lamar, the father of Gazaway, had married Rebecca Kelly in 1794, and the couple lived in the Sand Hills area outside Augusta, Georgia. Here Gazaway Bugg Lamar was born on October 2nd, 1798.

Not much is known about the early years and upbringing of Gazaway, but most probably he received a public school education as well as some home study. He most likely learned something of business from his father, who had been a charter member of the Georgia Steamboat Company. Although his father's interest in steamboats is most likely what led Gazaway into that area of business, Basil Lamar appears to have been a passive investor in Georgia Steamboat and was not active in the management of that company.

By the time his father died in 1827, Gazaway was 29 and already married, supporting a family and had active business interests in both Augusta and Savannah. He had married Jane Meek Creswell of Savannah on October 18, 1821. Any inheritance that his father Basil left was split among eleven children, so inheritance probably did not play a significant role in Gazaway's business beginnings. Unlike his father, Gazaway did not show much interest in owning and running a plantation. Most of his early business activities were centered on cotton brokering and acting as a commission merchant in Augusta, at first, and increasingly in Savannah as the years went by. As his cotton brokerage activities increased, he went on to expand his business activities into owning and managing a shipping business. This venture initially utilized pole boats and then barges and tug boats. By the late 1820s and early 1830s he was managing and had investments in the steamboats *Pendleton, Free Trade, Basil* Lamar, and *Governor Taylor.* As part of that business venture he had purchased wharves in Savannah. He also became involved in banking when in 1825 the Georgia legislature appointed him to the board of the Planter's Bank of the State of Georgia. Another bank with which he was involved was the Mechanic's Bank of Augusta, chartered in 1830. Gazaway's brother, George Washington Lamar, was cashier of that bank. In 1832 he held $3,200 worth of that bank's stock. By 1836 he was the second largest stockholder of the Mechanic's Bank, with an investment of $33,000.

Steamboat traffic in Georgia at that time had been controlled by the Steamboat Company of Georgia, which held a twenty-year monopoly. Although that monopoly was scheduled on paper to last through 1837, Gazaway had entered the business long before that. In fact, the monopoly rights were not strictly enforced because of the older company's financial problems and because of public outcry concerning its high rates.

Gazaway's increasing involvement with steam-powered vessels led him to experiment with the still very new and unproven iron-hulled steamships. Since he couldn't find a shipyard in the United States that could build what he needed, Lamar went to England, where he made contact with John Laird, who had been building iron steamships since 1829. They agreed that Laird would supply an iron ship in pieces, ready to be re-assembled in Georgia. The pre-fabrication of pieces rather than the purchase of a complete vessel was most likely related to import duties. On top of the cost of $30,000 there would have been an import duty due of about

$8,000 on a completed vessel. Lamar petitioned the United States Congress for relief, and in 1834 an act was passed to allow him to "import free of duty any iron steamboat with its machinery and appurtenances, for the purpose of making an experiment of the aptitude of iron steamboats for the navigation of shallow waters." In March of 1834 the pre-fabricated steamboat arrived, carried to Savannah in the hold of a British merchant ship. Because she had been fabricated in such a manner as to allow any reasonably talented shipyard to complete the construction, the task went smoothly. Within three months the ship was fully assembled at John Cant's shipyard in Savannah and christened the *John Randolph.*

The *John Randolph's* maiden voyage from Savannah to Augusta took less than 72 hours, an even more impressive feat considering that she did that while towing two other boats. Upon her arrival in Augusta, she was greeted by a large and enthusiastic crowd. Of critical importance to the citizens of Augusta as well as to Gazaway was the fact that just to the north over the South Carolina border a railroad had been established leading to Charleston. This upstart competitor presented a strong and serious threat to the established Augusta—Savannah trade. The new *John Randolph* offered Augusta and other inland Georgia towns along the riverways a fast and economical means of transportation to the deep water seaport of Savannah. This was critical to meet the competition of the new railroad that had been built to serve Charleston with its excellent seaport.

Proof of the success of the venture is found in twentieth century literature, specifically in a 1952 article in the *Georgia Historical Quarterly* by Alexander Crosby Brown titled "The *John Randolph:* America's first commercially successful steamboat." Even further proof of the success of this experiment and Gazaway Lamar's business ventures was the founding of the Iron Steamboat Company of Georgia in July of 1834. Most of Lamar's existing vessels were included in this venture along with the new John Randolph. By 1838 another iron ship, the steamer *Lamar* had been purchased from John Laird. In addition, Gazaway bought in his own name the *DeRosset* and the *Mary Summers,* which he later sold to the company. The success of these early shipping ventures provided a substantial portion of the foundation of Gazaway's increasing financial fortune.

In the early 1830s most trade between Europe and the South was routed through New York. G.B. Lamar felt that a more direct route was warranted that would cut out the Northern middle men. In spite of his attempts to establish a direct connection between England and the United States, he was unable to secure financial backing for the project in either England or the South. One brief trip to England in 1836 was enough to convince him to drop that idea. New York's domination would continue, and in due time Lamar would be attracted to the powerful economic center evolving there.

The enthusiasm for coastal steamship travel by passengers had been diminished by the explosion of the steamship *Home* off the coast of North Carolina. Public confidence in steamship travel was severely shaken, so Lamar and some fellow Savannah businessmen set out to build a steamship that would rebuild public confidence in steamers as well as turn a profit for the owners and investors. The steamship that they built was called the *Pulaski,* after the famed Polish hero of the American Revolution whose activities in and around Savannah were held in quite high regard. She was at the time the largest steamer in the coastal trade, with a length of over 200 feet. This elegant ship made a scheduled run from Savannah to Baltimore, with one stop in Charleston. Thus, the company was able to honestly make the advertising claim of "Only one night at sea." After the first three runs had been made and the revenues were not up to expectation, Lamar and his fellow investor John Hamilton attempted to sell her to the Republic of Texas. In a letter to his cousin Mirabeau Buonaparte Lamar, dated April 15, 1838, Gazaway wrote:

> Gen. Hamilton and myself used our best exertions to sell
> your Agent the Steamer Pulaski—but as the Boat was 40 or

$45,000 in debt, we could not have effected it without advancing that ourselves—which in addition to our previous interest in her (of 7000 each), would have borne on us onerously—I regret she is not in your country . . . It is very clearly ascertained, so far as our information goes, that you are to be the next President of Texas—I have script for some land, to whom shall I send it to have it well located—there are only 1600 acres of it.

I beg that you will not omit to give me the appointment of Consul for Texas at this port—it will give me some advantages here-and may do some good besides.

Always the wheeler-dealer, Gazaway had earlier sold the steamboat *Zavala* to Texas, but the Texans—for all Gazaway's efforts—never bought the *Pulaski*. His failure to sell her seems to have occurred either because some of the Savannah-based stockholders were unable to make up their minds, or more likely (as G.B. Lamar had claimed) because the price was not high enough to cover the outstanding debt. In either case, something held up the sale of the *Pulaski*.

While the negotiations were stalled for the moment, G. B. Lamar took his family, including his wife, seven children, and his sister Rebecca on board the *Pulaski* for the trip to Baltimore. One source quoted at the time claimed that they were on their way to England to see Queen Victoria's coronation. Since she is listed as having been Queen from 1837 to 1901 they were either very late, the coronation was later than the start of her reign, or the report was inaccurate. The first leg of the trip from Savannah to Charleston went smoothly, but on the night of June 14, 1838, off of the coast of North Carolina, a boiler exploded and blew the ship into several large and many small pieces. Those lucky enough to have survived the explosion had mostly floating remains to cling to. A few made it to lifeboats and were able to get to shore. Of the Lamar family, the only survivors were Gazaway, his sister Rebecca, and his son Charles.

After the explosion, the *Pulaski* quickly broke into two sections. The group on what remained of the forward section used ropes and timbers to lash the wrecked remains together and thus formed a raft. Twenty-two survived from this group after spending four days at sea in the blistering sun, knee-deep in seawater without food or drinkable water. The wind had pushed them almost to the beach, but just as their hopes of making land grew, the wind shifted and they were pushed back out to sea. They were finally saved by the schooner *Henry Camerdon,* whose captain, upon spotting them afloat, yelled out, "Be of good cheer. I will save you." As soon as they were brought aboard, the parched survivors rushed for the water keg, but the captain ordered a guard around it! This wise and knowing captain then had half-pint portions of water laced with molasses doled out to revive and strengthen them. The survivors told the captain that others were in the sea, afloat, so they began a search, and thus the aft half of the wreckage was recovered with four people aboard, including Charles A.L. Lamar and his aunt Rebecca. After the explosion, twenty-three people had crowded on that part of the wreck, Mrs. Lamar and her children among them. It was later reported by a Mr. B. W. Fosdick of Boston that when he reached the promenade deck, there was a yawl being launched that was full of women and children, including G. B. Lamar's wife and small children. Since the wreckage of that portion of the promenade deck was sinking, the yawl was partly on the deck, which was quickly becoming awash, and partly in the ocean. Several men, including Gazaway Lamar, were holding the boat steady in the hope that it would float clear as the wreckage sank completely underneath it. Mr. Fosdick grabbed the bow to help hold it upright, but the deck sank so quickly when hit by a large wave that the yawl quickly took on water until it was swamped. The same wave pulled Fosdick under, causing him to lose his grip and be swept into the ocean. Another passenger, Mr. Eldridge of Syracuse, remained on the deck and later advised Fosdick that nearly all the passengers in the yawl, including Mrs. Lamar and her children had been lost after the boat had been swamped.

After two days of drifting, the survivors on the stern section made a decision to send six men, including Gazaway Lamar, to shore in a small boat. After four and a half days of rowing, the boat reached safety at the New River Inlet at Wilmington, North Carolina. Mr. Fosdick ended up aboard a piece of the wreckage of the ladies' cabin and made it to the safety of shore after several days.

The ship that had been built to instill public confidence in steamship travel had failed completely in that respect. The *New York Times* ran a short article about the Pulaski accident in 1877, just after G. B. Lamar died. Titled "An incident in the life of the late G.B. Lamar," the article briefly told the story

> The deceased Gasaway [*sic*] B. Lamar, late of this city, whose death a few days since was noticed in THE TIMES, was one of the survivors from the wreck of the ill-fated Pulaski which sank off the coast of North Carolina June of 1838. On the night of the wreck he managed to get his wife and eight (sic) of his children into one of the steamer's boats with the intention of following in company with his son, afterward, Col. C.A.L. Lamar, when a wave swept the boat and its precious freight out of their reach. The father and son succeeded after almost incredible hardships in reaching the shore in safety but the mother and her eight little ones were never afterward heard of.

Another view of this explosion and its survivors comes from Fanny Kemble, the British actress, who published a diary titled *Journal of a Residence on a Georgia Plantation*. She relates the tale of James H. Couper, scion of an old Georgia planter family whose father had properties on Sea Island and St. Simon Island. Couper was travelling aboard the *Pulaski* with his sister and another woman, along with their children and a maid. After a night of dinner and dancing, they retired, but were soon startled by a loud explosion. Going immediately onto the deck, Couper found that everything was in total confusion, with people running about and the ship starting to list. He went to the ladies' cabins, advised them of the urgency of the situation and told them to dress and meet him on deck at once which they did. Several life boats were launched, one with only two sailors in it. Couper told first one and then the other lady to jump into the boat. Couper, carrying one of the children, then jumped but hit his foot on the gunwale, throwing him into the water. He quickly got back into the boat and ordered the sailors to start rowing while he steered. All around them they could see furniture and other wreckage to which people were clinging for their lives. Slowly another boat full of survivors moved away from the wreckage, and they all watched as the splintered hulk of that once mighty vessel slipped below. Those in the boats rowed through the night, and when dawn broke they were able to see the surf crashing onto the beach. Certain that they would never make it through the surf to the shore without capsizing, they continued to row through the day in the blistering sun in the hope of finding a safe place to land. The sailors who were rowing claimed to be exhausted, but Couper urged them on and promised that if safe landing was not discovered by nightfall they would risk the surf and head for the beach. All of them had witnessed another boat, carrying eleven passengers, overturn on its way through the surf; only six of those passengers made it to shore alive. All that long hot day they kept rowing while searching for a safe place to land.

Finally, when the sun started to go down, Couper told the men to rest before attempting to make the landing through the surf. After some time, they turned their boat to the line of breaking waves and headed for shore. They made it safely through one, then another line of waves. Finally, an oar somehow dipped into the foaming surf, throwing them off line. Immediately they were caught by a breaking wave; the boat spun around, and the passengers were thrown into the foaming water. Couper quickly surfaced and made a head count, finding that all but a Mrs. Nightingale were safe. She was nowhere to be seen, but just then Couper felt something brush his leg under the water. He dived under the surface, where he was able to locate and save the frightened woman.

Her child of less than one year, who had been wrapped under her dress, was still with her and also safe. With Couper's urging, they all were able to drag themselves to shore. Cold, hungry, and wet, they huddled in the dunes until they finally found a farmhouse and shelter. Mrs. Kemble relates that many of the leading Georgia planter families lost kin in that tragedy, since it was in fashion for many of the wealthy households to repair to Saratoga and Newport during the hot summer months.

Out of this disaster there came one tale noteworthy for its happy and romantic ending. A young man named Ridge had spied a pretty young thing while they were both getting on board and hoped to have a chance to meet her. Somewhat shy, he hadn't had the opportunity to make any headway in that regard by the time of the explosion. He was helping several men launch one of the boats when he spotted the young lady. He started off after her in the hope of getting her to board the boat with him, but he lost sight of her and, in spite of a fervent search, she was not to be found. Returning to where he had helped launch the boat, he found that it was gone. He soon had no choice but to go into the water, where he lashed several settees together with a bit of old sail and a cask to form a makeshift raft. When Ridge noticed a survivor thrashing in the water he left his raft swam to save the survivor, who proved to be the young lady of his attentions, a Miss Onslow. Naturally, he pulled her aboard his raft. The makeshift heap of flotsam was hardly suited for two, but when she offered to leave he refused to let her go. Later, a small but overcrowded boat appeared and invited her to join them, but this time she refused to leave him alone. Together they worked to increase the size of their little raft, and during their ordeal they made a pledge to each other that they would never separate if they were lucky enough to survive. The two were the last to be saved, and when they were finally on firm ground, Ridge offered to release Miss Onslow from her pledge. He told her that all his worldly possessions had been lost on the *Pulaski* and that he was now destitute. His future wife would hear nothing of the sort, saying that the worst threat that poverty offered was nothing compared to what they had just survived. Poverty probably never became an issue, since it was reported that she later disclosed to her then-husband the happy news that she was the beneficiary of an inheritance of several hundred thousand dollars.

All told, only 59 out of a reported 183 passengers and crew survived that tragic night. After this bitter tragedy, Gazaway not surprisingly appeared to became more religious, but this fact did not turn him away from continuing to build his wealth. In addition to his other enterprises, he had recently purchased the toll bridge over the Savannah River at Augusta, so an income flow was assured from that source as well as other investments. That his new-found religious fervor did not slow his continued attention to his business ventures is seen in another letter to Mirabeau Buonaparte Lamar, dated November 9, 1838. Here Gazaway again mentions the script for the 1600 acres, then complains that no reply to the letter of April had been received. Gazaway goes on to allude briefly to the wreck:

> You will have heard long before, of my sudden and great afflictions—You may (as I did formerly) suppose that I have consequence of them being estranged from my right reason—But believe not such—They are suggestions of the Devil . . . Nor was I frightened into this change nor brought to it by despair at the time. I never despaired while in the utmost danger, with no visible means of escape and all reasonable chances in the proportion of ten million to one against me. Nor did I perceive any change in my mind or feelings at any time during my danger—Nor until I was some days on shore . . . Endeavor to humble your heart—and to serve God with reverence and sincerity, and you cannot fail to be a better Man and a better Ruler . . .

The letter ends with a request to be appointed Consul for the Republic of Texas at the port of Savannah " . . . if you have no better offer."

One year and one month after the tragic loss of much of his family, Gazaway married Harriet Cazenove of Alexandria, Virginia. Gazaway built what was described as a "substantial house" in the Sand Hills area near Augusta, but continued to live in Alexandria for some time.

7

G. B. LAMAR:

The South's Wall Street Banker

Restless for new ventures, Gazaway was finding that neither Savannah nor Augusta could hold his attention for long. He was ready for New York City, and by 1846 he had made the city (more or less; his actual dwelling was in Brooklyn, then a separate municipality) his home. Through his previous dealings as a cotton broker and shipowner, he had established extensive contacts in New York and probably felt quite at home there. For the first several years he was involved with cotton brokering, shipping corn and flour to England, buying and selling wheat and apples, and investing in ships, including the *Warren,* the *Dirigo,* the *Ericsson,* the *North American,* the *Miantonome,* the *Ann Hood,* and the *Richard Cobden.* The latter ship was to eventually play a part in the activities of Charles A.L. Lamar, Gazaway's son who had also survived the shipwreck.

By 1850 Gazaway had either tired of the cotton business or sensed problems ahead in that market and proceeded to substantially cut back on his activities in that commodity. He now directed his substantial energies toward an activity of which he also had a fair amount of knowledge: banking. He believed that New York's growth in both population and business offered a profitable opportunity in banking, since the number of banks had not kept pace with the growth of the city. Lamar and some associates founded the Bank of the Republic, with $1,000,000 in capital. The headquarters was established at the corner of Wall Street and Broadway, which was considered to be quite a good location at the time. Lamar was chosen by the directors to be the president and, not surprisingly, the bank soon gained a reputation for its dealings with planters, businesses, and governments of the American South.

When the State of Georgia contemplated selling bonds, Lamar advised Governor Howell Cobb (whose wife was Mary Anne Lamar) that if the bond's coupons were payable in New York, foreign investors would be attracted, since they commonly had agents in New York who could collect the dividends for them. Again, when the Georgia legislature voted to approve $525,000 worth of bonds, they were marketed by the Bank of the Republic at more favorable terms than the state had received on its previous issue, which had been sold in Georgia. Howell Cobb was happy with the transaction, as was the legislature, which voted in February 1854 "That his Excellency the Governor be and he is hereby requested to transact all banking business of the state, in the sale of bonds, payment of interest, or otherwise, he may have in New York, with the Bank of the Republic of that City."

A few years later, when the market for state bonds had dropped sharply, then-Governor Johnson had Lamar buy back some outstanding bonds that were selling at a discount, but in a confidential manner that insured that no one would know that the state was the buyer. Although completely legal, Johnson was concerned that the state's reputation with investors could be harmed if they learned of the state's purchase of the discounted bonds. Lamar was able to buy the bonds and maintain the confidentiality, an act that had the effect of keeping the state as a customer of the bank.

By 1855 Gazaway had resigned as president of the bank, but he retained his seat and his influence as one of ten directors. His good friend James Soutter replaced him as President.

Along with his business activities, Lamar, most likely still strongly influenced by his tragic loss of family, was quite generous in his donations to charitable causes, especially religious ones. The Georgia Episcopal Institute received 800 acres outside of Macon for its headquarters, and various other religious institutions, including African American churches were beneficiaries of his largesse.

In 1856 Gazaway was asked by a group of Savannah businessmen to help in founding a new bank in that city. He agreed, and the directors elected him president of The Bank of Commerce. He held this position until 1860, although he continued to reside in New York for much of the period.

Another venture in which Gazaway became involved was a fertilizer company dealing in guano from an American source, and thus not subject to the high prices demanded by the Peruvian government monopoly, which controlled much of the international market. Just as his attention was being taken by this new venture, his friend James Soutter fell sick, and Lamar resumed the presidency of the Bank of the Republic.

It was at that time that a scandal arose, and Lamar and Soutter were called before Congress to testify about the bank's knowledge of some missing bonds that belonged to the government but had shown up in the account of one of the bank's customers, a firm by the name of Russell, Majors and Waddell. The bank's customer had a contract to transport military goods, but Congress couldn't authorize payment until the job was completed. Russell, Majors and Waddell, financially squeezed, persuaded an Interior Department clerk to give them negotiable bonds, held in trust for Indians, in return for promissory notes. When the bonds ended up on the market, Congress found out and ordered a full investigation. The Bank of the Republic had been used by Russell, Majors and Waddell for many of the transactions, and thus came under investigation. The Congressional committee found that the bank had acted properly and exonerated its officers of any wrongdoing. Although this crisis passed, other troubles were brewing on the horizon.

Lamar's pro-Southern bias caused the bank to experience increasing difficulty, especially by late 1860 when he made public his belief that the South had a right to secede. He had long believed this to be the region's right, but he had also long believed that going to war to maintain that right would be a lost cause and not worth the cost.

With Lincoln's victory over Douglas, Lamar became convinced that the new President and the Republican party, dominated by abolitionists, would be completely against Southern states' rights. Seeing no alternative, he added his voice to those who talking secession. When a group of New York businessmen formed a group to convince Southerners that they should not bolt from the union, Lamar refused to join them. At about the same time, a "free city" movement was started that called for New York City to get out of the Union. Because of the secrecy practiced by the founders of this group it has been speculated, with no good proof, that Lamar may have been involved in this effort. Lamar's beliefs were clearly stated in a letter he wrote to Alexander Stevens of Georgia, on December 4, 1860: "Let the South go without hesitation and delay . . . Now is the time."

Actions always speak louder than words, and Lamar acted by being the intermediary in the quite legal, open market purchase of ten thousand U. S. Army muskets for the state of South Carolina. He also helped the state of Georgia in the shipping of five thousand Army muskets. As these activities of shipping arms to the South became known, controversy ensued. By the end of 1860, the Governor of New York, Edwin Morgan, banned the shipment of arms from New York. In January of 1861, Morgan ordered the seizure of 38 cases of muskets aboard the ship *Monticello* by the state police. D.C. Hodgkins & Sons of Macon, Georgia, owned 10 cases, most likely under contract to the state of Georgia. Upon notification of the seizure, Georgia's Governor Brown demanded that they be released and turned over to his agent, Gazaway Lamar. An immediate reply was requested, and when none had arrived three days later, Governor Brown ordered ships in Savannah harbor belonging to citizens of New York to be held. When Lamar received word of the seizure he advised Brown that the release of the muskets was about to happen and that the ships should be released. Governor Brown followed Lamar's advice and released the ships, but when the New York authorities failed to deliver the cases, another seizure of ships in Savannah was made. This time Governor Brown's move worked and the muskets were released.

In Montgomery, Alabama, a convention was under way, with Howell Cobb presiding, to establish the Confederate States of America. Lamar was still convinced that war would mean bloodshed and that the secession should be done in a friendly way. Gazaway Lamar wrote to Cobb and suggested that the money in the New Orleans mint should be exchanged to repay the North the costs of Fort Sumter in Charleston and Fort Pickens in Pensacola. "An attack on Ft. Sumter . . . would be very disastrous if any blood be shed," Lamar wrote.

For a brief period of time between the formation of the Confederacy and the outbreak of the Civil War, G.B. Lamar, still living in New York, was able to help the new Southern government. On one occasion the new government wanted to issue bonds but couldn't find engravers capable of the work. Lamar was able to get the job done in New York. Not long after that, the Confederate Secretary of the Treasury requested that Lamar have the engraved plates sent to him, but the Federal authorities seized them before he could send them. The New York engravers, in a display of loyalty to their customer, had defaced the plates before handing them over to Federal authorities. (In order to address the shortage of engravers in the South, the Confederate government eventually had a group of qualified men brought in from Scotland on a blockade runner. When the runner was attacked and ran aground, they were forced to take to the small boats to make it safely into Wilmington, North Carolina.)

With the outbreak of actual hostilities, Lamar's usefulness to the South as a New Yorker became severely limited. He would have left New York even sooner than he did, but his wife was too ill to travel. Harriet Lamar died on May 3, 1861, and Gazaway B. Lamar returned to his beloved Georgia soon after her death.

8

GAZAWAY BUGG LAMAR:

Hospitals, Banking, and Blockade Running

Back in Savannah, too old to serve in the military, Gazaway Lamar had again been voted in as president of Savannah's Bank of Commerce. Along with this work, he threw himself into several war-related activities including serving on a three-man committee to organize volunteers for Savannah's defense, helping to get a gunboat for the "Ladies Gunboat Fund of Savannah," and supporting the construction of a floating hospital for soldiers. In addition he served as army paymaster.

By June of 1861 he had traveled to Atlanta, where he was chosen as head of the Confederate banking convention. The second meeting of that group was held in July of 1861 in the new capital, Richmond. This was a time of rampant optimism for supporters of the Southern cause, since it immediately followed the lopsided victory over Northern forces at First Manassas (also known as the Battle of Bull Run). Lamar was able to visit the battlefield and meet with some wounded Georgians. Many if not most Confederate supporters in those days were brimming with hope and the belief that the South, having started on the road to victory, would be able to conclude the war in its favor and do so quickly. Lamar, who had long worried that the Southern states could not work closely together and would thus eventually lose, had allowed the glow of victory, at least for the time being, to bring him to the belief that the South could win this war in reasonably short order.

Also basking in that glow of the victory at Manassas were the other assembled bankers, who passed a resolution stating "That it is the opinion of this meeting that the capital resources of the country are abundantly adequate to supply all the demands created by the war." This statement indicated that they were in agreement with the Government's borrowing in the form of bonds as a sound method of financing a war. In other words, they expected or hoped to see the war end quickly, since borrowing against non-existent assets can never continue indefinitely. Later however, as reality set in, Lamar and the other the bankers would come to the opinion that the continual issuance of bonds and printing of money, without the tax revenue to repay the loans was leading the Confederacy to inflation and financial chaos.

In May of 1862 G. B. Lamar became president of the Bartow Hospital of Savannah and changed its name to the Georgia Hospital. The stated policy of the hospital was to be open to soldiers "without money and without price." A great deal of Lamar's time was spent in fundraising and dealing with volunteers in addition to heading the bank and being involved with the Confederate bankers.

Influenced by his extensive experience as a cotton broker, Lamar believed that cotton was a safe wartime investment, especially with inflation raging as government printing presses worked around the clock producing currency. In a letter to the wife of Dr. Rees in May of 1862 he stated, "I know nothing better in these uncertain times." Not only did he buy cotton and take cotton in payment for guano, but he attempted to interest English investors in buying cotton to be held in interior Southern areas in sheds protected by high fencing and identified as British property. At the end of hostilities the cotton was to be sold, and Lamar would receive one quarter of the profit. Only one merchant, Henry Lafone of Liverpool was interested, and 1400 bales were bought and stored for him at Montgomery, Alabama.

As long as the cotton was behind the Union blockade it was frozen money; non-working capital. Since the war was now going on longer than he had originally envisioned, Lamar began laying

the plans to form Georgia's only large blockade running corporation to get some of that cotton out and sorely needed goods back
in. Up until that time he appears to have owned partial interests
in the ships *Emma, St. Mary,* and *Nina,* all blockade runners. In
August of 1862 he contracted with the *Emma* to ship out 100
bales of cotton. Before reaching the open sea, she ran aground and
was burned by her fleeing crew. The St. Mary, or at least the rights
to her, was bought while she lay under water on the contingency
that she could be made to float. After attempting to bring her to
the surface for several months, the effort was abandoned and the
offer to buy her was canceled. A group headed by Lamar bought
the *Nina* from her Charleston owners for $50,000. On the first
voyage out she got 320 bales of cotton to Nassau and loaded up
with $30,000 worth of goods. Months went by without any word
of her, but the owners finally learned that she had been lost in a
storm. In spite of the loss of both the ship and her return cargo,
proceeds from the sale of the cotton cargo exceeded the entire cost
of the venture and paid a small dividend.

Convinced that the Confederacy would have difficulty sus-
taining a long war due to the poor financial condition of the government as well as the effects of the blockade, Lamar started to
lobby for negotiations with the North while the South still had a
strong hand. The summer of 1862 had seen military victories for
the Confederacy in the Shenandoah under Stonewall Jackson and
at Second Manassas under Lee. In addition, the Union forces were
encountering problems, especially with McClellan's Peninsula
Campaign. Convinced that the time was right, Lamar wrote a long
letter to President Jefferson Davis. In it Lamar laid out his beliefs
that the high water mark of Southern military success had been
reached, and that the South's ability to continue to wage war was
weakening.

"Our resources are being exhausted," he wrote, and the
Treasury's ability to continue to float bonds was weakened. Further damage would make obtaining supplies an even greater problem. The peace negotiations, even if rejected by the North, would

be heard in Europe and possibly help the Southern cause there. Also, Lamar anticipated that a Southern peace offer would receive notice due to the 1862 Congressional elections. Although, in hindsight these arguments appear to have been quite timely and with great merit, they failed to move Davis toward peace negotiations. This was one of over two hundred letters that Lamar wrote to the Confederate government, with little visible effect. The one exception was in the area of fiscal matters, where his experience was most valued. Secretary of the Treasury Christopher Memminger and Lamar worked together and were in agreement on many matters. Over the years, however, Lamar became upset with Memminger, among other things for his inability to control counterfeiters. Tension increased when Lamar agreed to buy $300,000 worth of cotton bonds in mid-1863. Before the deadline for the offer, Lamar telegraphed Memminger, changing his offer to only $36,000. Due to wartime interruptions, Lamar's order to change the total was not received by the deadline, and Memminger insisted that he take the original amount. Lamar refused until Confederate Attorney General T.H. Watts declared that he had an obligation to do so, and Memminger brought suit. Lamar relented and bought the full amount in order to forestall legal proceedings. Another area for disagreement was the "cotton embargo." Several Southern leaders, Lamar included, believed that cotton could provide the financing needed to support the war effort. Others, including Memminger, believed that by withholding cotton from the market and keeping it in the South, the Europeans would pressure the North into lifting its blockade. When Memminger interfered with Lamar's efforts to export his privately-owned cotton, Lamar became outraged.

With the prospects for a negotiated peace or quick victory greatly diminished, Lamar's efforts to run the blockade were expanded. In the spring of 1863 Lamar and nine other men announced the formation of The Importing and Exporting Company of Georgia. The name has an interesting ring, but it was far from unique in that it most probably was inspired by the well-known and successful Importing and Exporting Company of South Carolina. As the Union blockade of the Southern States tightened, the South was suffering increasingly from shortages of goods necessary both for daily life and to support the war effort. Early in the war, blockade runners had been able to make huge profits, but the risks had substantially increased as the Union Navy tightened its grip on the ports of the Confederacy. One of the first Union blockaders had been an armed tug boat, the *Uncle Ben,* which was soon captured by the Confederates and renamed the *Retribution.* Subsequent additions to the Union blockade fleet were more substantial and successful in seriously curtailing shipping to and from the South. Since both Gazaway Lamar and his son Charles had long owned interests in ships, and since Charles had previously invested in slave blockade runners, it was a natural step for them to become involved in blockade running with commercial goods; Gazaway Lamar's previous involvement with blockade runners must have certainly made him aware of the risks involved. Both father and son owned substantial quantities of cotton, and the blockade had put cotton in short supply and thus valuable in Europe. In the South cotton could be bought for three cents a pound, while it could be sold in Liverpool for forty-five cents a pound. There was enormous profit to be made in both directions of the trip through the Union blockade. On the outbound voyage blockade runners carried cargoes of cotton to English mills that were starved for raw material. For the homeward voyage the runners loaded up with guns, shoes, and a wide range of consumer goods that were always in short supply and thus very valuable in the South. Aside from the profit motive, there was also a patriotic reason to run the blockade, since the Confederate government relied almost exclusively on privately-owned blockade runners to supply both the war effort and most of the day-to-day needs of the population.

For all these reasons, the Importing and Exporting Company of Georgia came into being. Not long after the very first announcement of the company's formation, another announcement followed, stating that several million dollars had already been raised. One

month later the announcement was made that all the stock was
had been sold.

Good ships were in very short supply and very expensive in
the Confederate States. To solve this problem Capt. Henry
Hartstein, who had headed a naval expedition to the Arctic, along
with Charles A.L. Lamar, Gazaway's son, were sent to Europe to
buy one or more steamers. The requirements for these ships were
the ability to carry at least three hundred and up to one thousand
bales of cotton, to be speedy, and to be registered in a neutral
country. Because of this last requirement, Lamar is not identified
in the many books on the blockade running era, nor is the Importing and Exporting Company of Georgia listed as owning blockade
runners. One book, however, Stephen Wise's 1988, *Lifeline of the
Confederacy*, documents the Georgia ownership of his boats. In the
earliest days of the blockade, large oceangoing steamships had been
able to depart England and sail directly to deep water southern
ports such as Savannah. When the increasing strength of the Union
blockade put an end to that practice, the larger ships were sent to
interim ports such as Nassau and Bermuda. There, the cargo was
loaded onto fast, shallow-draft steamers for the 500- to 600-mile
run to Charleston, Wilmington, or some other suitable port. A
type of boat that had been developed for use in the waterways
around the British isles, known as a Clyde steamer, was soon found
to be highly suitable for this work. Alterations were made, including removal the staterooms in order to increase cargo space and
thus make the ships more useful as blockade runners. When the
limited supply of ships available for purchase had been depleted,
new ones were built specifically as blockade runners. The most
common design was a steel-hulled vessel with twin paddle wheels
propelled by steam engines, a draft of eight feet or less, and low
profile above the deck. The combination of shallow draft and low
profile allowed them to run along the beach just outside the surf
line while blending in with the background of sand dunes and
coastal hills. Good Welsh anthracite coal was used because it burned
with a minimum of attention-getting smoke. Since the South lacked

the ability to build such ships, and since the British were already building them, most of the fast blockade runners were English built—and quite a few were English owned.

Young Charles A.L. Lamar found London a difficult place in which to do business for a Southerner hoping to buy ships. The blockade had drastically increased the demand for ships suited to the business, and prices had responded accordingly. Vessels that had been ordered months earlier at a cost of £13,000 were selling for £20—25,000 as they neared completion. English investors in general were not optimistic about the prospects for Confederate success in the war, and thus few were interested in investing in Southern business ventures. This meant that the company would most likely have to put up much if not all of the purchase price in cash or gold. The ship-buying mission suffered another setback with the sudden death of Captain Hartstein from a stroke in September of 1863.

Finally Charles' efforts paid off in a contract with a Liverpool merchant, Henry Lafone. Charles was also fortunate to locate a qualified technical advisor to replace the deceased Captain Hartstein. The new expert was C.A.L. Lamar's friend and in-law of sorts, John Newland Maffitt, whose sister was the widow of Mirabeau B. Lamar. It would have been difficult, if not impossible to locate a more qualified candidate for the job of technical advisor than Maffitt. He was a "salt" of a sailor who had been born at sea in 1819 in route to the United States. He is quoted as having stated, "Since I was born a son of old Neptune, I was duty bound to offer my allegiance to the sea." In the days before there was an institution called the Naval Academy, a friend of his family obtained for him a commission as a midshipman, and at age thirteen in 1832 and he started his Navy career aboard the sloop-of-war *St. Louis*. Following that duty, he was stationed in the Mediterranean, and in 1838 became a "Passed Midshipman" (more or less the equivalent to ensign today). His service had continued in various Atlantic Coast posts until early in 1842, when he was posted to the Coast Survey. In later years he would have plenty of opportunity to use the extensive, intimate, and invaluable knowledge of the coastline, especially the vicinities of Charleston and Wilmington, that he gained in that post. When the Civil War broke out, Maffitt returned to Washington, and like so many sons of the South who were in the service of the United States armed forces, resigned his commission. While awaiting the shipment of his possessions from Washington to a new Southern address he was shocked when a friend's whisper warned him of his pending arrest. That information was enough to prompt him to immediately depart (with the help of a friendly Union officer) by way of Long Bridge on the night of May 2, 1861. He never did regain his possessions nor receive compensation in spite of continued attempts after the war. One report states that his lost property was valued at over $70,000.

The Confederates initially put him aboard the so-called "war ship" *Savannah*, which was nothing more than a converted coastal freighter. Maffitt left little to the imagination in his description this ship: "A more absurd abortion for a man-of-war was rarely witnessed." Eventually, after several interim postings, including as Naval Attache to Robert E. Lee, Maffitt was assigned to the *Cecil*, a blockade runner under contract to the Confederate Government. She was then docked in Wilmington, North Carolina, and years later Maffitt told the story of that first run through the blockade which was published in the *United States Service* magazine in 1882:

> In silence Fort Caswell is passed, and a dim glimpse of Fort
> Campbell affords a farewell view of Dixie, as the steamer's
> head is turned seaward through the channel. The swelling
> greetings of the Atlantic announce that the bar is passed;
> over the cresting waves the good craft swiftly dashes, as if
> impatient to promptly face her trials of the night. Through
> the settled darkness all eyes on board are peering, eagerly
> straining to catch a view of the dreaded sentinels who sternly
> guard the tabooed channel. Nothing white is exposed to
> view; every light is extinguished, save those that are hooded
> in the binnacle and engine room. No sound disturbs the

solemn silence of the moment but the dismal moaning of
the northeast winds and unwelcome, but unavoidable, dashing of our paddles . . . Instantly out of the gloom and spin-
drift emerges the somber phantom form of the blockading
fleet. The moment of trial is at hand; firmness and decision
are essential for the emergency. Dashing between the two at
anchor, we pass so near as to excite astonishment at our non-
discovery; but this resulted from the color of our hull, which,
under certain stages of the atmosphere, blended so perfectly
with the haze as to render the steamer nearly invisible . . . a
broad-spread flash of intense light blazed from the flag's
Drummond [light] for in passing to windward the noise of
our paddles betrayed the proximity of a blockade runner.
"Full speed" I shouted to the engineer. Instantly the increased revolutions responded to the order. Then came the
roar of heavy guns, the howl of shot, and scream of bursting
shells. Around, above and through the severed rigging the
iron demons howled, as if Pandemonium had discharged its
infernal spirits in the air. . . .

Maffitt and Cecile came through that night safely, and he went on
to run the blockade on board her and aboard the Nassau numer-
ous times until May 1862, when he was posted as captain of the
Confederate raider *Florida*. This new command had been bought
in England, and sent out unarmed to Nassau. After legal maneu-
vers in Bahamian courts to block her departure had been defeated,
Maffitt moved her secretly to an out-of-the-way anchorage and
had her guns brought on board and mounted. Because the rammers
and other tools needed to operate the guns had been shipped sepa-
rately, it was impossible to operate the newly installed armament.
Defenseless and short-handed, they set sail from Bahamian waters, but yellow fever ravaged the crew, including Maffitt and his
son, who was fatally stricken. To get *Florida* properly fitted out
and manned, Maffitt plotted a course for Mobile, Alabama, where
a desperate run brought her into the harbor under heavy fire from

the blockading Union ships. By January, *Florida* was finally ready to sail, with working guns, a full crew and orders to disrupt enemy shipping. In spite of his recognition and treatment by the Confederate people as a hero, he continued to hold the rank of Lieutenant. After evading six gunboats during a day-long flight in departing Mobile, *Florida* went on a long cruise, capturing and burning Union ships. The war prizes that she captured were burned because there was no safe port to bring them to. On a swing to Brazil, Maffitt received the news that he had been promoted to Commodore. By the end of that summer, with *Florida* requiring repairs, they sailed for Brest, France. After much red tape, permission was granted for the ship to remain in port and be repaired. Rumors were rampant in the French populace about the "bloodthirsty pirates," rumors that may have been created by Union agents. To allay these fears, a copy of the ship's log was printed in the local paper, possibly at Maffitt's request; that appears to have satisfied everyone except the Union agents. Before *Florida* was again ready for sea, Maffitt suffered a heart attack at age 42 and took a leave of absence from the navy. It was thus that John Newland Maffitt was in Europe and able to give technical advice to Charles A.L. Lamar about the kinds of ships that the company was contracting to have built as blockade runners.

An agreement was made to acquire the *Lilian*,* and subsequent dealings with the Englishman Henry Lafone resulted in the Importing and Exporting Company owning part-interests in four steamers. Negotiations by another agent resulted in the purchase of another two ships. Unfortunately, one problem after another frustrated the best attempts of the company to make a profit. The near-disaster that marked Charles A.L. Lamar's return to the Confederacy aboard the blockade runner *Ceres*—referred to in the story of L.Q.C. Lamar—offered an indication of things to come.

Of all the things that were to hurt Lamar's blockade running company, the states' rights argument that had been at the very root cause of the war between the states was to grow into the issue that caused the company impossible difficulties. The Confederate

Congress passed a bill in February 1864 allowing the President of the Confederacy to regulate blockade runners. Jefferson Davis decreed in March of 1864 that one half of all cargo space on privately-owned vessels had to be reserved for Confederate cargo. Soon afterwards, Lamar's company chartered some of its vessels to the State of Georgia in hopes of evading the 50% restriction. The governor was in full agreement, but in the next month, as the first boat was to set sail, the Confederate authorities refused to release her. Upon appeal, the Confederate leaders insisted that the boats were still private in spite of the lease arrangement to the state, and thus still subject to the regulation. Not giving up so easily, the state governors went to the Confederate Congress, but legislative relief was vetoed by President Davis.

So there sat the first of the company's blockade runners. *Little Ada* was bottled up in Charleston harbor, held in by Confederate as well as Union guns. In June, with no other option, the *Little Ada* sailed from Charleston with 50% of the cargo hold containing Confederate cotton, which earned the Import and Export Company of Georgia some freight revenue but had no potential for profit. That system proved to be so devoid of profit potential for ship owners as to be unworkable, especially in a wartime situation where not only were boats subject to enemy shelling and seizure, but also where the shipping channels were littered with unmarked wrecks, causing even further wrecks.

The *Lilian*, another Import and Export ship, had been built by the Thompson shipyard in Glasgow. She had a steel hull boat with a forward "turtle back" deck and two raked smokestacks. She was rated at 150 tons and claimed a speed of 15 knots. Like many blockade runners, her captain found the port of Wilmington to be an attractive destination. It was close to the heart of many Confederate military operations, especially Lee's army in Virginia, and had good railroad connections to Richmond. Most important, however, Wilmington offered unique and very direct access to the ocean. It is situated on the Cape Fear River, with a narrow strip of beach separating river and ocean. A hurricane had opened up a deep water entrance through the barrier beach, appropriately called New Inlet. To protect traffic through the inlet, the Confederates had constructed the very effective Fort Fisher of palmetto logs, railroad ties, and sand bags. Not very far away, at a distance of about nine miles, was the main entrance to the river. At this entrance was an old, unused fort named Fort Caswell, which the Confederate forces had rebuilt and used very successfully. Offshore, between the two inlets, lay Frying Pan Shoals, the existence of which made it necessary for the blockading Union boats to sail in an arc of fifty miles to get from one inlet to the other. Because the coastal beach sloped gently and uniformly, blockade runners developed the practice of sailing to the coast about thirty miles or so from either inlet, and then turning to run parallel to the beach barely outside the surf line where they were certain of sufficient depth. Also, the pounding of the surf masked their noises, and the dunes made their low profile and light gray paint very difficult to see. Fort Fisher offered protection for a range of five miles, thanks to her English Whitworth guns, which were often needed to keep the Union gunboats at a distance.*

Using the distance covered by the fort's guns for a head start, generally on a moonless, stormy or otherwise murky night, and always with a bit of luck, blockade runners successfully slipped into and out of Wilmington. Because the Union boats had to travel a long distance to refuel, either to Port Royal or Beaufort, their standard practice was to conserve fuel by keeping minimal steam up. The captain of a blockade runner knew this, and would sneak as far as possible, in absolute silence, until detected. Then, upon the first hint of detection the runner would be ready to use one or more of a variety of hot burning fuels such as turpentine laced cotton or bacon fat for maximum and instantaneous steam and thus speed. Once detected, the captain of the runner no longer worried about producing any tell-tale smoke or noise, and the order to the engine room was full power, and damn the consequences. That fat-fueled quick burst of speed before the Union boats had a chance to bring their boilers up to full steam often gave the blockade runner that few minutes needed to slip out of or into port. Daring captains, fearing an inability to run the surf line, developed yet another trick that was commonly used. They would silently slip their blockade runner in between the Union boats, ever so silently in dark or fog. The strictly-adhered-to order of the day was to maintain absolute silence. To achieve this they would cover the paddle wheel boxes with canvas, and the men on deck took to wearing slippers when walking about on deck. When finally detected, they would rush at full speed for the protection of the fort's guns or the open sea. Because of the proximity on both sides of other Union boats, the blockaders often would not fire out of fear of hitting their comrades-in-arms, and thus they were forced to watch helplessly as the runner slipped through their formation.

On her initial run out of Bermuda to Wilmington, Lamar's *Lilian* was under the command of none other than Commodore of the Confederate Navy, John Newland Maffitt. Due most probably to Captain Maffitt's quite public fame (in Europe especially), a correspondent of the *Illustrated London News* was on board. His story was published on July 16, 1864 in the *News*, and it detailed the *Lilian*'s maiden run of the blockade into Wilmington. (A report of that voyage also appeared in the *London Telegraph*, written by Mr. Francis Lawley. This report contains several examples of identical wording and many phrases very similar to those used in the *Illustrated News* story—a similarity that would lead one to suspect either two names used by one author or a case of rank plagiarism.)

> Upon the evening of Wednesday the 1st of June, the Lilian and the Florie, two of the fleetest and most beautiful of the blockade defying vessels, started simultaneously from Bermuda upon the first trip inward which either had ever made. Both belong to the same company, but there is an emulation between the two rival vessels which is not satisfactorily allayed by their experience hitherto, but which waits the solution of further trial. The weather was lovely, the sea like

a milldam, and favorable beyond expression to light draught
and gossamer craft, such as are these blockade runners, which
lightly scratch the surface instead of clutching the ribs of old
ocean, and which in summer seas have no more to fear from
heavy sea going craft, like the Rhode Island or the
Vanderbuilt, than has the Irish night express from the lum-
bering freight train which leaves Euston Square five minutes in its rear. Rarely have two more attractive prizes slipped
through the meshes of the blockade than the two vessels of
which I am writing . . .

About 350 miles out they spotted a sailing ship that the captain
thought might be on fire, and Maffitt stated, "The ship which
leaves a companion at sea in distress must be accursed." It turned
out to be a Union steam assisted sailing ship under full steam,
blowing billows of smoke in an attempt to chase another blockade
runner. Upon discovering this, Maffitt commanded the *Lilian* to
be set back on her original course. When the day dawned the third
day out, Captain Maffitt hove-to between the outer and inner
rings of Union blockade boats to await nightfall, but before the
welcome dark arrived, the U.S. Navy made its appearance early in
the afternoon.

Then the tall masts of a large Federal cruiser, and her immense paddlewheels and lofty black hull were visible, and
for the first time, as our antagonist approached us from the
direction of Wilmington, the 'airy fairy Lilian' prepared to
give us assurance of that speed which we all felt she possessed. Some slight delay there was before steam could be
fully got up, and for some twenty minutes our pursuer
seemed to gain upon us. But as the pressure of steam as-
cended from fifteen pounds to twenty, from twenty to
twenty-three, from twenty-three to twenty-six, and as the
revolutions of the paddle mounted from twenty-six to
twenty-eight, from twenty-eight to thirty-three per minute,

the 'Lilian' flew out to sea swift as arrow from a bow. In little
more than two hours the hull of our pursuer was invisible,
and her topgallant sails a speck upon the distant horizon.
6But as she still lay between us and Wilmington, it became
necessary to run around her. This also the light-heeled 'Lilian'
had little difficulty in accomplishing, but as the sun dropped
into the sea, and our pursuer, although distant, still hung
upon our rear, we found, that reckoning little the speed of
our advance, we had sighted the inside blockade squadron
before the close of day. There was nothing for it but to
persevere, and fortunately before we approached close to
land, darkness had completely set in. Silently and with bated
breath we passed cruiser after cruiser, distinctly visible to
every eye and suggesting the flashing out of a blue or
Drummond light, and the rush of grape shot and shrapnel
through our rigging and bulkwards. But it was not destined
upon this occasion the 'Lilian' should receive her baptism of
fire. Just as we approach Fort Fisher a dark spot is seen on
the bar. It is a Federal launch, seen by us too late for Captain
Maffitt to indulge the anxious wish of his heart and to run
her down. We pass her within twenty yards, and again the
expected volley of musketry is wanting. Another moment
and we are under the Mound upon which stands the fort
and eagerly questioned for news. The news is good all
around. 'Three times three for General Johnston, six times
six for General Lee; and in mirth and laughter the night
wears away. Three hours after us comes the Florie, and is
heavily fired at as she wears inwards. But morning finds
both vessels and their cargoes safe at the wharf in Wilmington,
nor is it rash to predict for them both the probability of
many returns.

The next month, *Lilian* made a run from Bermuda to Wilmington,
now under the command of an Englishman by the name of Daniel
Martin. On board were three Confederate navy officers, including

Lt. W.P. Campbell who had gained fame by getting to "test" the boilers on the *Rappahannock*, a former Royal Navy sloop-of-war that the British had sold to the Confederacy. Diplomatic pressure had prevented the British from allowing the *Rappahannock* to leave port, but Campbell was able to convince the British that before he could authorize payment he needed to inspect her to test the engines. They agreed to let him test the engines by steaming out onto the Thames. This he did with the shipwrights still on board getting things finished. Although they protested as the landmarks they knew so very well fell from sight, he kept right on steaming, out the mouth of the river and across the channel to France, which offered total freedom. Campbell became quite of a hero for that daring feat of gallant action.

Upon leaving Bermuda, the *Lilian* threaded her way out of the dangerous shoals surrounding the island in daylight and under the watchful eyes of a Union patrol. When the captain had her in deep water, still in Bermudan territory, he waited for darkness. Finally at night *Lilian* successfully slipped away from the Union patrol and headed for Wilmington. She was nearing the mainland coast and as so often happened to runners this late in the war she was spotted and chased by a blockader, the U.S.S. *Shenandoah*. A barrage of withering gunfire was let loose by the Union ship. Shells were hitting the water on each side, and on board *Lilian* the three Confederate Navy officer passengers called out the time between the puffs of smoke from her guns and the impact of the shells. Only the action of the waves was helping *Lilian* by giving her enemy an unstable platform from which to fire. The Captain ordered the Confederate mail burned, and then had rifles thrown overboard to lighten her weight. The situation looked serious enough that he ordered the Confederate flag stuck. Upon hearing that order, the Confederate officers, who by then had donned their Navy uniforms, wouldn't allow it, as they were afraid that would put them at risk of being declared pirates. A large explosion suddenly shook them and the *Lilian* immediately slowed. One of her steam engines had been hit and put out of commission. The captain then went to his cabin, and Lt. Campbell took command of the ship. Immediately, the chief engineer reported to Lieutenant Campbell that *Lilian*, having been especially designed as a blockade runner, had the ability to easily detach the drive shaft from one of the paddlewheels and thus permit her to operate with only one engine. The Captain ordered the engineer to proceed with the necessary work to disconnect the damaged engine, and within minutes the ship was underway again. Next, Captain Campbell changed course and turned her into the wind. This maneuver allowed the *Lilian* to evade the *Shenandoah*, which was sail powered. With the immediate danger under control, one of the crew reported that "Captain Martin" was in his cabin, dead drunk and with an empty bottle beside him. Approaching Fort Fisher in the haze, *Lilian* passed through a line of Union gunboats, who, as luck and the hope of the captain would have it, initially mistook her for one of their own. A Union captain soon realized from her shape that *Lilian* was a blockade runner, and hailed her to heave to or be blown out of the water. The Lilian's commander responded, "Aye, we will stop the engines," and announced that he was heaving to. As the Union boat slowed to lower her longboats, *Lilian* was ready to respond: Campbell had previously called to the engine room for full speed. He pushed her as fast as he could with only one engine, and they were able to make it to safety under the range of the guns of the fort. The log of the *Shenandoah* for July 30, 1864 details that chase into Wilmington:

> At 3:45 PM sighted a steamer burning black smoke to eastward; made all sail in chase. At 4:30 PM made stranger out to be a double smokestack, sidewheel steamer, apparently a blockade runner standing to the northward and westward. At 5:45 he showed rebel colors. Called the first division and powder division to quarters and began to fire at her with the 30 and 150 pounder rifle Parrott. At 6PM beat to quarters and fired all the divisions. At 7 PM took in top gallant sail and foresail. At 7:30 took in foretopsail. During the chase

fired 70 rounds from 30 pounder Parrott, 55 rounds from
150 pound Parrott, 18 rounds from XI inch guns, and one
round from 24 pound howitzer.

On departing Wilmington, the *Lilian* successfully evaded the blockaders at the mouth of the river and made her way out to sea. Her
pilot, J. W. Craig, described that day as follows:

> Trouble began before we got outside. An armed barge from
> the United States fleet had come close inside the western bar
> and lay in our track in the channel, and immediately upon
> our approach sent up a rocket and fired a gun, which was
> instantly answered by the fleet outside, and I remember we
> crossed the bar in a bright flash of Drummond lights and
> rockets which made the night as bright as day.
> Every one of the blockaders was firing at or over us so we
> headed out to sea, and when the next morning, Sunday,
> dawned we had just succeeded in dropping the last of the
> cruisers, which had chased us all night.
> We were congratulating ourselves after breakfast that morn-
> ing that we would have a clear sea towards Bermuda-and,
> by the way, the sea was as smooth as glass-when the lookout
> in the crow's nest reported a vessel of war ahead . . .

They had unfortunately come upon the Gulf Stream Squadron,
and the chase went to half past one in the afternoon. A shot that
had hit below the waterline had crippled her, and despite efforts
to plug the leak with blankets and other bulky material, *Lilian*
took on so much water that she slowed, and could no longer be
steered. Soon, the Union forces captured her.

"Although every effort had been made to escape," Craig continues, "those of us who knew Captain Maffitt, the former commander of the Lilian regretted very much his absence on this occasion, as he would most likely have been more fortunate in getting
away."

On board were five Wilmington pilots, bound for Bermuda where they were supposed to meet up with more returning blockade runners. They told the capturing Union sailors that they were ship's firemen and deckhands, and thus were able to eventually escape. Naturally, if their captors had as much as a suspicion that they were really pilots ready to bring more runners from Bermuda over the Wilmington bar, they would have been in Union prisons until the end of the war.

By late in 1864 the Union blockade had been so tightened and improved that it consisted of three different layers. One was well off shore in the Gulf Stream, standing between the Confederate mainland and both the Bahamas and Bermuda. Another lay off the shore of harbors such as Wilmington some forty or fifty miles out, and a third was very close in to Wilmington's two inlets. The Importing and Exporting Company of Georgia, when it finally was able to get started in business owned nine ships. Of these, four ended up being captured, two were wrecked after having made several runs, and three never even made it into a Confederate port. Their first boat, the *Little Ada* made but one voyage out before she was captured on the way back to Charleston. She was captured by the Union blockader *Gettysburg*, itself a war prize which had started as a blockade runner named the *Margaret & Jessie*. Under the name of those two ladies she had been a very successful runner that had made eighteen runs before being captured and renamed by the Union forces. *Lilian* ran the blockade successfully five times, making her one of he most successful Lamar ships. She was caught by the Gulf Stream Squadron while leaving Wilmington for Bermuda with a cargo of cotton. The less successful *Nina* foundered and was captured on her second run to Charleston. *Emma Henry* made one trip into Wilmington and was captured on the way out in December of 1864. Two others were wrecked. They were the *Florie* (sister ship of *Lilian*) which ran aground on a sunken hulk near Wilmington. Another "successful" boat, she had completed six successful trips. *Little Hattie* made between four and eight successful voyages to Nassau. Of the three remaining steamers, *Flora III* never made it into Charleston, running aground off of Fort Moultrie in December 1864. The *Susan Bierne* also never even reached a Confederate port. She sprang a leak on the way to Wilmington in December of 1864, and returned to Bermuda. The last, the *Mary Bowers* was found hung up on the wreck of the *Georgiana* in an entrance channel to the harbor of Charleston. The Captain of the Federal frigate *Wabash* discovered the *Mary Bowers* and reported that "the vessel is undoubtedly lying on the wreck of some vessel, as there is deep water all around her. Being almost entirely submerged, it is impossible to save anything from her. Her bell marked 1864, her binnacle and compass, and two kedge anchors are saved, also a small quantity of liquor and a few signal flags."

With the continuing and relentless pressure of the Union blockade, it was little surprise that by the end of 1864 the Importing and Exporting Company of Georgia was $100,000 in debt, and its stock was worthless. Much of the South was in the same state at that point of the war. It was just about at that time that Sherman was marching through Georgia, and the advance of Union forces soon halted whatever was left of the company's remaining operations. One by one, the blockade runners' favorite ports had been closed. In September of 1864 Gazaway Lamar had warned in a letter to Confederate Secretary of the Treasury George Trenholm that "Blockade running must be abandoned unless we can get some safe harbor." Trenholm certainly recognized that fact. As a partner in Fraser and Trenholm, shipping agents for the Confederate States, his own company was heavily engaged in the blockade running business. It is believed that Trenholm's South Carolina company owned the *Hattie*, about which at least two interesting stories exist. The first is a colorful story that details a very rare daylight run by the *Hattie* into Wilmington in October of 1864. *Hattie* was running for Wilmington, and upon spotting Union boats ahead, her Captain declared that if they were to go down, they should do so gallantly. He ordered all bunting and flags to be flown, including the Fox and Chicken, the ship's personal flag. Rooftop observers in Wilmington saw her run through the outer circle of eight Union steamers, which fired what appeared to be a curtain of steel. Closer in, having outrun the outer group, *Hattie* approached a pack of thirteen gunboats waiting at the harbor mouth. The Fort's cannon opened a hole in that group, and *Hattie* made a high-speed dash into the inlet and in to safety. It was reported that *Hattie* was one of only two ships that ever made successful daylight runs into Wilmington. *Hattie* made one final run at the very end of the war, earning her the likely honor of being the last blockade runner to make it into and out of Charleston. In February of 1865, Captain Lebby slipped her through the outer ring of twenty ships, and as she neared the inner line of gunboats they opened fire. For fifteen minutes the Union ships guns blazed until *Hattie* ducked into a small channel near Fort Sumter. There she came upon two barges full of Union troops who opened fire with their rifles. The intense gunfire wounded several of *Hattie*'s crew including the pilot, who lost several fingers on the hand that grasped the ship's wheel. Passing out of range of the troops on the barge, *Hattie* then came upon a Union monitor that was so close that Lebby could hear the orders to fire being given. This time *Hattie* got past without being hit. Upon arriving at Charleston, Captain Lebby found it to be under bombardment, so he quickly off-loaded his cargo, re-loaded and fled for Nassau. On the outbound voyage they counted 26 blockaders, past all of which they were able to slip quietly without attracting any gunfire. *Hattie* remained safely in Nassau until hostilities ceased.

On Christmas Eve 1864, Union forces attacked Fort Fisher, which guarded the inlet to Wilmington, NC, but withdrew after their Army forces under General Ben ("The Beast") Butler, called it a day after what some called a poorly planned and executed effort. The General had relied on the explosion of a boat full of gunpowder to blow open the fort, but the explosion simply made one great big noise. The man in charge of the supporting naval forces, Admiral David Porter, kept his fleet at Fort Fisher and lobbied hard with the powers that be for another assault. He wrote to the Secretary of the Navy and General Grant, among others. The

Union armed forces returned two weeks later, and this time the Army was led by General Alfred Terry. The bombardment started at eight and went on until two o'clock. When the bombardment stopped, eight thousand men with twelve days' provisions, arms, and digging tools were sent ashore. The fleet kept up the bombardment on January thirteenth and through the fourteenth. On the fifteenth, at about 3 P.M., the final assault began. The fort, over a mile long and built of palmetto logs and sand, formed a series of traverses that were essentially a string of connected gun positions. Nine of these traverses had been taken after bitter hand-to-hand combat before darkness fell. The remaining troops defending the battery were led by Colonel Lamb who, realizing that he could no longer withstand the vastly overpowering force, finally capitulated. The Confederate fortifications, consisting of 169 artillery pieces manned by 112 officers and 1,971 enlisted men, fell to the enemy, and all the survivors were taken prisoner. Many had died, and others had escaped.

No longer would Wilmington provide Lee's army with the Enfield rifles, gunpowder, shoes, medicine, and many of the other necessities that this port had provided for much of the war. The loss of the port of Wilmington, coming two months after the fall of Savannah to the advancing forces of General William Tecumseh Sherman, all but sealed the fate of Lee's Army of Northern Virginia.

9

GAZAWAY BUGG LAMAR:

Swearing Lincoln's Oath

General John Geary, U. S. Army, had been placed in charge of Savannah as military governor by the conquering Sherman. General Geary invited the citizens of the conquered city to take an oath of allegiance as proclaimed by President Lincoln on December 8, 1863. The proclamation had been authorized by Congress and called for citizens of the Confederate States to take an oath of allegiance to the Constitution of the United States. In return for taking the oath, all property rights would be restored to that individual, excepting of course the right to own slaves.

Forced to choose between continuing his allegiance to a clearly defeated although still feebly resisting Confederacy and taking an oath of allegiance and thereby salvaging his property, Gazaway Bugg Lamar made the pragmatic—and in reality the only viable—choice. After all, he was sixty-six and not in the greatest of health. To continue the fight would almost certainly have cost him much if not all of his substantial fortune. So, on January 6, 1865, he took the oath as required by the President and Congress. Since the oath didn't require him to support the Union war effort, "it was no hardship to resume allegiance to it," as he was quoted in the *New York Times* on January 28, 1866. His logic was spelled out in a letter he had written, and in spite of it having been marked "To be opened when I am dead," the letter was printed in that newspaper while he was very much alive, and said, in part, that "Sherman with 60,000 or 70,000 men, armed and equipped superior to any army in any war in any country prior to this, had devastated the whole course of his march from Atlanta to Savannah . . . had joined the troops on the Atlantic coast, supplied with abundance of provisions and ammunition, was ready to march northward without any adequate force to resist him."

As a successful and well-known businessman and public figure, Gazaway realized that his previous, very open support for the Confederacy, along with his great wealth, required that he follow the terms of the oath very closely or risk jeopardizing his chances for recovering property. He cooperated with Sherman and Geary, and even asked for Geary's help in getting letters through the battle lines to his son and nephew. These letters asked them join him in taking the oath. His son Charles, the red-bearded firebrand whose own adventures in the war era are worthy of note, not only refused to go along, but appears to have strongly and adamantly disagreed with his father's position. This reaction caused Gazaway to write the "To be opened when I am dead" letter for posterity, explaining in great detail his thinking and his very candid and personal feelings. Unfortunately, this letter, which explained with emotion and in great detail his strong support of the Confederacy, was captured by Union troops and subsequently printed in the *New York Times*. The printing of the contents of this letter was to become just one of many problems that were to arise for Gazaway Lamar (along with many citizens of Dixie) following the fall of the Confederacy.

The property that Lamar was working so hard to save consisted of real estate as well as a substantial amount of cotton. Of the thirty-five thousand bales of cotton that Sherman had captured in Savannah, Gazaway had an interest in at least three thousand. That March, Union forces sent a total of thirty-eight thousand bales of cotton to New York, where they were sold at auction and the proceeds held by the Treasury. Eligible owners were required to file claims to the government in order to recover any money due them for their cotton.

In addition to the loss of this cotton, Lamar's warehouses were held by Union forces, and he was denied the use of them. Ware-house timbers had been used for firewood, his private papers and those of the Bank of Commerce had been seized, and troops were quartered in his home.

"Much of my furniture, china, and glassware, and all the bed linen, and a large majority of my library have been removed, sto-len, and sent off I know not where. Some whiskey, sugar, hams, and five boxes of wine . . . only horse . . . fine milk cow . . ." com-plained Lamar in a letter to President Lincoln in February of 1865. Lincoln, busy with greater matters, sent no response to this letter.

The assassination of Lincoln two months after Lamar's letter caused a frenzy of activity in Washington to establish a connection between Booth and Confederate or other southern leaders. Some-how, during the investigations, the name Lamar had been men-tioned in the testimony of someone being investigated. Since no statement or accusation was being taken lightly or left uninvestigated in those dark days, Secretary of War Edwin Stanton directed his assistant, Charles A. Dana, to arrest Gazaway B. Lamar!

Gazaway was pulled from a sick bed in Georgia and brought under military guard to Washington. No charges were filed, but Gazaway was held for three months at the Old Capital prison under less than comfortable circumstances. The cell was a small room holding fourteen men, far beyond its designed capacity. The climate was neither good nor healthy, nor was there was no oppor-tunity for exercise.

All attempts to gain an interview with President Johnson fell upon deaf ears until late in July when a Boston attorney, Henry Durant, husband of Lamar's niece, wrote to Gazaway that Johnson "was friendly, confidential in his manner and spoke kindly of you and said he had no doubt if you returned South you would be an ardent Union man as anyone." On July 28, Johnson released Lamar on parole. The investigation proved that the "Lamar" in the "testi-mony" was a total fabrication.

Upon his return home, Lamar found that matters there had gone from bad to worse. Treasury agents and military officials had joined forces to seize the books of the Importing and Exporting Company of Georgia, along with his personal papers. This allowed them to easily locate and seize cotton stored in Alabama, Florida, and other parts of Georgia. General J.M. Brannan had taken over command in Savannah, and he and Lamar clashed. Brannan believed that Lamar deserved punishment for his role in the war. Lamar believed that he had complied completely and openly with Lincoln's proclamation and was due all the legal rights of any United States citizen.

In an attempt to right the wrongs that had been put upon him by an oppressive government, and to stop the Treasury agents from stealing his cotton, Lamar set up a visit with President Johnson. Lamar was referred by President Johnson to Secretary of Treasury Hugh McCulloch, who advised Lamar that the Treasury agent in Savannah, Mr. A. G. Browne, had authority only to seize only Confederate cotton and not any that was privately owned. With Lamar still in the office, the Secretary ordered Browne to be telegraphed to return Lamar's cotton and to report back to the Secretary in Washington.

It was a small victory for Lamar, but the battle continued. Back in Savannah, Gazaway learned that some of his warehouse property had been turned over to a person suspected of being in cahoots with Brannan. Lamar went to Brannan's boss, General Steedman, who stated that he had not instructed the taking of any of Lamar's property and ordered Lamar's property returned to him. At the same meeting, Lamar got Steedman's written permission to remove eight hundred bales of cotton from a warehouse in Thomasville, Georgia.

Upon the conclusion of the meeting, Lamar and his nephew and namesake G. B. Lamar Jr. proceeded to Thomasville. The district commander insisted that the pass also had to be signed by Brannan, although it had already been signed by Steedman, Brannan's commander. The paperwork was then sent to Savannah for Brannan's signature. During the delay as they waited for Brannan to sign the order, Lamar journeyed to Florida in a futile attempt to recover seven hundred bales of cotton that had been taken from him by Treasury and military officials. The deeds and paperwork that proved his ownership were ignored, and the corrupt officials kept the cotton. Upon his return to Georgia he learned that A.G. Browne had been replaced by his son, A.G. Browne Jr., who was involved, in conjunction with one William Beard, in the seizing of cotton owned by the Importing and Exporting Company of Georgia. Lamar tried to halt this with a legal action on the part of the local sheriff, but Baird brought in some black soldiers, forced the sheriff out of the way and carried off the cotton.

Frustrated by the illegal seizures in Florida and Georgia and correctly convinced that the Treasury officials were corrupt, Lamar made a huge and costly mistake. In his frustration and anger, he wrote to his nephew to convey an offer of a bribe to A.G. Browne Jr. Although the nephew refused to deliver the letter, he did not destroy it, and this letter was later discovered, unopened. The contents of this letter eventually proved to be a ticking "time bomb" for Gazaway Bugg Lamar.

The eight hundred bales of cotton from Thomasville were eventually moved by Lamar's actions but without the permission of Brannan who had never signed the order approving the move, even though his superior had previously done so. Upon learning that the cotton had been moved, Brannan ordered the cotton seized and both G.B. Lamar and G.B. Lamar Jr. arrested! A search of the papers of G. B. Lamar Jr. by the Union agents led to the finding of the still-sealed letter from the senior Lamar addressed to, and offering a bribe to, United States Treasury Agent A.G. Browne. The charge of conspiracy to bribe a U. S. official was added to that of theft of government property (Lamar's cotton). It was at the time following his arrest that Lamar's letter, sealed in an envelope marked "To be opened when I am dead" was published on the second page of the *New York Times* under the heading "The following document was found among the papers of G. B. Lamar of Savannah, now on trial in that city for stealing cotton, and for attempting to bribe the United States Treasury agents." The newspaper article took up one whole column of the paper. In the letter, Gazaway stated that he had been living in New York when the secession took place, that he was a member of the Nullification party, and "I preferred Nullification as the rightful remedy for all unconstitutional enactments by Congress." He went on to state that

> I adhered to the Confederacy, and gave it free and liberal support, and I am prepared to show that directly and indirectly I have expended between $300,000 and $400,000 for it . . . I could, if justice and law were dealt out to me in common with others, preserve all my property to myself, pay off all my debts, and have a comfortable competency remaining for myself and family, and I could whenever I pleased, expatriate myself from Yankee dominion and vicinage. By refusing, all my property must go into the Yankee Treasury under their confiscation acts . . . If I can not serve the Confederacy by the course I have adopted, I can at least defeat the Federal Treasury in acquiring all my property for its advantage . . . I intend it (this letter) mainly for my children when I shall be cold in the grave, but I am not insensible to the good name I would desire to leave behind me and therefore hope it will be published at a proper time for my vindication before all the people of the Confederacy and all I ask of any to whom it may come is to deal fairly with the facts and circumstances and to distinguish between the unanimity and enthusiasm of the whole people of the Confederacy in 1861 and the reverse of those in 1865.
> I censure no man here; I mean only to vindicate myself, and while I protest against a judgment of myself without a hearing, I would judge no man without hearing his defense.

The military tribunal that had been formed by Brannan, who strongly disliked Lamar and who believed that Lamar's wartime record made him deserving of punishment, had conviction as its only goal. In spite of Lamar's ownership of the cotton in question and in spite of weak testimony on the part of the prosecution, the predisposition of the tribunal along with these two damning letters led to Lamar and his nephew being found guilty. They were fined $25,000 each and sentenced to three years in jail.

In the year that had passed since the end of the war, Lamar's prospects had gone from bad to worse and were now very bleak indeed. Gazaway had been arrested on the basis of groundless rumors after Lincoln's assassination and held in jail in Washington without ever being charged of any crime. Much of his property had been stolen by corrupt carpetbaggers. Most of his cotton had been seized by Sherman's Army, sold by the government, and the money retained by the Treasury. Finally, he had been tried by a military tribunal, and a large fine and a jail term hung over him pending an appeal to President Johnson. Failure of that appeal would almost certainly cause Lamar to lose any legal right to claim compensation for the property that had been seized by Sherman's Army. As things stood, the Court of Claims had taken the position that anybody who had given aid or comfort to the rebellion was ineligible to receive compensation for seized property claims. Since Lamar would not be so foolish as to deny having given comfort or aid to the Confederate cause, he refused to apply to the Claims Court. The only basis in fact for Gazaway Lamar's claim rested completely on the terms of his oath in accord with Lincoln's proclamation.

A necessary step to winning the claim was to prove ownership of the seized property. To do this it was necessary to gain possession of his papers and documents, which were held by the Treasury Department. The legal battle dragged on through 1867 and 1868. In the late 1860s Lamar brought suit against Charles Dana and A. G. Browne for damages related to false imprisonment and to recover thousands of bales of cotton. Although he had little chance of winning, Lamar used those trials to call attention to the injustices that he had suffered since taking Lincoln's oath. Those cases were eventually dismissed on the legal basis that the defendants were acting as agents of government and could not be held personally liable.

Finally in 1869, after years of disappointment, the tide started to turn. Charles Jenkins was former Governor of Georgia and a friend of President Johnson, who, in the waning days of Johnson's administration (Johnson had been impeached, but won his trial and served a full term), was able to get the President to act on the matter of Lamar's appeal of the conviction by the military tribunal. In February of that year Johnson rejected the findings of the tribunal and decided in Lamar's favor. That cleared one very major hurtle, but the bias of the Claims Court was still against any Southerner. This was all the more true in the case of Gazaway Lamar, who had given aid and comfort to the Confederacy through a wide variety of actions that had been publicly documented.

Gazaway hired a New York law firm to present his claim for over one million dollars to the Court of Claims. Although he was still barred from receiving compensation, two important Supreme Court decisions were soon to remove that obstacle. In *The United States v. Padelford*, the Court held that in the Claims Court a proof of oath was "a complete substitute for proof that he gave no aid or comfort to the rebellion." As soon as this finding came down the members of Congress, free from any strong Southern vote, passed the Drake Amendment nullifying the legal finding in the Padelford case. Two more years passed before the Supreme Court found the Drake Amendment to be unconstitutional and thus upheld *Padelford*. A joyful Lamar was warned by his attorney not to celebrate too soon, since the size of his claim was so large that it was likely to attract unwanted attention.

The unwanted attention came in the form of H. Boardman Smith, representative from New York, who brought the subject up in Congress. Both Lamar and the Supreme Court were targets of the Congressman's wrath. Lamar, complained the Senator, was about to receive money without any say-so on the part of Congress in spite of his having been one of the leading blockade runners of the war. Representative Young of Georgia attempted to set the record straight where Boardman had erred, and a general debate followed. After extensive debate it was concluded that the legislature should not interfere with the Supreme Court and the Court of Claims.

The time had finally come to celebrate. The Court of Claims on January 2, 1873 made the largest individual award of the post Civil War-era, $579,343.51. When the Justice Department appealed, Gazaway felt that he needed even more help and retained Massachusetts politician and former Federal general Benjamin Butler—he of the failed assault on Wilmington—to assist on the case. Another year passed before the Court rejected the Justice Department's appeal and finalized the decision in April of 1874.

The amount granted was only about one half of what had been claimed. When Gazaway's lawyers inquired about the difference between the amount claimed and the award, they were told that this claimant should be satisfied, since his was the largest personal judgment ever awarded. In 1990s dollars this amount probably equals something between $10 and $50 million.

With his last major battle won, Gazaway Bugg Lamar was free to live out his life in peace with the knowledge that he had overcome the forces that had been out to deprive him and his family of their property. Unfortunately, time for this enjoyment was short. In October of 1874, just six months after winning the final appeal, he died at the age of seventy-six.

After a funeral in New York from the home of his daughter, Mrs. Robert Soutter, Gazaway Bugg Lamar was buried in Alexandria, Virginia. His will contained an interesting bequest, brought on by his humanitarian feelings. He left what was a grand sum in those days of $100,000 for the purpose of setting up a Negro hospital in Savannah.

10

CHARLES AUGUSTUS LAFAYETTE LAMAR:

Slave-Blockade Runner

In reading the exploits of Charles Augustus Lafayette Lamar, one is reminded somewhat of the fictional Rhett Butler in *Gone With the Wind*. Both were blockade runners out of Savannah but this Lamar had the advantage of being the son of the very rich Gazaway Bugg Lamar of Augusta, Savannah and later New York. Contemporaries described Charles, born on April 1, 1824, as a large red-headed man, and his outspoken manners earned him the descriptive title of "firebrand."

His second middle name, Lafayette, is said to have came from his being baptized in the arms of the Marquis de Lafayette when that Revolutionary War hero was in Savannah and Augusta in 1825. General Lafayette had been accompanied on part of his trip through Georgia by Governor Troup, and Troup's confidential clerk, Mirabeau Buonaparte Lamar, was a member of the party that traveled with Lafayette for several days after greeting him in Savannah. The baptismal story, mentioned in a book on the family, is quite probably accurate, since Mirabeau Lamar was in a position to have requested that Lafayette hold his cousin's child during the baptism (another Lamar, Henry Greybill Lamar, accompanied Lafayette through Alabama on this same trip). Evidence of early use of the Lafayette middle name is found in C.A.L.'s family bible, which has a handwritten inscription inside the cover, "Charles A.L. and Caroline A. Lamar, from their uncle George W. Anderson." Inside that bible on the births page is listed "Charles Augustus Lafayette Lamar." Lafayette, on his triumphant tour of the country whose freedom he fought for, was the type who would probably have readily agreed to hold a baby during baptism, yet another favor at yet another public event.

C.A.L. Lamar's father, Gazaway Bugg Lamar, had started out in Augusta, and expanded his business operations to Savannah starting in 1823. Thus, it is most likely that the family moved there sometime in the 1820s. In 1825 G. B. Lamar was appointed by the State as a director of the Planter's Bank in Savannah, and his shipping activities in Savannah started at that same date.

Little is known of the early years and family life of Charles A.L. Lamar. he was fourteen when the signal event of his young life occurred, the explosion and sinking of the steamer *Pulaski* with the loss of his mother and six siblings. One can only imagine that Charles and his father (who had survived with him) became closer after the tragedy. After his father's remarriage, a letter from Gazaway reports that Charles, now sixteen, was said to be attending school in Alexandria, Virginia, where Gazaway had moved as it was the home of his new wife.

When the senior Lamar decided to move to New York in 1846, he appointed Charles to look out for his Savannah business interests that included wharves, warehouses, a rice mill, and a cotton brokerage as well as shipping interests.

But in addition to his father's interests, Charles had business dealings of his own. Charles' attempts to convince his father that the United States' 1808 ban on the importation on "new" slaves was incorrect fell on deaf ears. Charles set out to find his own investors to back his slave importation ventures, which promised cheaper labor and higher profits than the "closed" domestic market. Young Charles, red bearded and reportedly something of a hot-head, was convinced of his "right" to go to Africa for slaves.

In a letter from Gazaway B. Lamar to John B. Lamar dated

October 16, 1858, the senior Lamar is clearly not in agreement with his son. "I am not on Charley's side in the controversy . . . but he is so impulsive, & so crazy on that Negro question—that I can make no impression on him."

In July of 1857, Charles Lamar's ship, the *E.A. Rawlins*, was seized by Federal agents as she readied for a trip to Madeira. The supplies she carried seemed to indicate that she would be used in the slave trade, but since the possession of supplies did not clearly prove that intent, Lamar made a successful protest to the Secretary of the Treasury and the ship was released. A run was made to Madeira, and the ship returned to New Orleans, apparently without slaves. On the next trip, however, the supercargo, a man named Postell, took unauthorized control of the ship and stranded the captain Eben Sears on the small island of St. Thomas, several hundred miles from the mouth of the Congo. Two months later the *Rawlins* showed up in Savannah without cargo and without proper paperwork from a port of departure. Again she was seized, but with no evidence of slave running available, she was released.

Lamar was also rebuffed in his attempts to get permission for another ship, the *Richard Cobden*, to bring in what he described as African emigrants as "passengers." The Secretary of the Treasury, Howell Cobb (married to a Lamar), refused Charles permission on the basis that no state would admit them as free men and thus they were clearly slaves.

With his actions under close scrutiny and repeatedly thwarted by the Federal government, Charles took a new tack intended to make his actions less visible. A group led by Charles Lamar purchased the schooner *Wanderer*, a fast and elegant pleasure yacht built for a wealthy sportsman and New York Yacht Club member, John Johnson.

The *Wanderer* had sailed from New York to New Orleans and back in 1858, stopping in Charleston, Brunswick, and Key West along the way. Upon her return to New York, the announcement was made of the sale of this fast, good-looking boat to William C.

Corrie of Charleston. His announced purpose was to go on an extended cruise with a group of his rich friends.

Before clearing New York harbor, *Wanderer* was hailed and detained by a revenue cutter under suspicion of being a slaver. The next day she was inspected and thought to be innocent, since she didn't appear to be carrying the type of cargo typical of slavers. Revenue agents looked for but didn't find the telltale signs that would indicate the preparations of a slave runner: bedding material, larger than normal cooking and water supplies, lumber, guns, handcuffs, and money. The 15,000 gallon water tank that had been recently added was explained as necessary for long-range cruising, and the food supplies were found to be fine meats and wines. Lacking the appearance of a slaver, and thus any intent to break the law, the *Wanderer* was released and immediately sailed for Charleston.

While in Charleston, two significant events took place. Corrie went to the British Consul and asked for British protection for his yacht and guests, which was granted. The importance of this action was that British ships of war often patrolled the African coast to stop slavers. Paperwork from a British diplomat requesting protection probably would improve, and in no way harm, the chances for friendly treatment of the *Wanderer*. The second thing that took place was that supplies needed for feeding and restraining slaves were brought aboard. There could be no question about the *Wanderer*'s mission.

Corrie told friends that he was off to Port of Spain to inspect an estate. Upon arriving there, he told people that he was off to visit the island of St. Helena to see Napoleon's final resting place. Instead of St. Helena, the *Wanderer* ended up at the mouth of the Congo, a hotbed of slaving activity. Corrie and his crew pretended to be rich yachtsmen on a pleasure voyage, even inviting the officers of a British man-of-war aboard for dinner. Although the British officers laughingly refused when they were invited to inspect this luxury yacht to insure that she was not a slaver, the British Captain later reported to London in his official dispatches that *Wan-*

derer was indeed a slaver. Not aware of the written reports to London which proved that the British correctly suspected the true intent of the *Wanderer*, Corrie took pleasure in repeating the story of how he had fooled them. By the time the United States Navy vessel *Cumberland* showed up, her captain was told by the British that the *Wanderer* had departed several days earlier, carrying a cargo of slaves.

Another American gunboat, the older and slower Vincennes, had spotted the *Wanderer* as she was leaving the coast, but she soon gave up the chase as she was clearly unable to catch the fast, sleek yacht. Once out of sight of the coast, the threat of interception was minimal since both the American and British naval patrols stayed close to the coast, especially near the mouth of the Congo.

From October 23 until November 29 the *Wanderer* crossed the Atlantic, eventually landing at Jerkily Island, Georgia. When their signal to the Cumberland lighthouse for a pilot went unanswered, Corrie and another man went by small boat to the lighthouse, where they found Hereto Harris, the assistant lighthouse keeper. Harris agreed to take them to James Clubb, a qualified pilot and the full-time lighthouse keeper, who was at that time on Jekyll Island. Clubb demanded the very high price of $500 to bring the slaver safely to the Jekyll Island landing, and the island's owner, John Dubignons, paid him with a note for that amount. Chubb's extraordinary fee is clear evidence that he understood the illicit nature of the ship's business.

After the contraband humans were off-loaded, the *Wanderer* was moved to a more secluded spot upriver where she was cleaned and stripped of most, if not all, of her incriminating gear. Charles *Lamar* was notified that she had arrived, and the next day the steam tug Lamar set out, supposedly for Fernandina, Florida, to pick up cedar wood. With Charles Lamar aboard, the tug started off in the direction of Florida but stopped instead at Jekyll, where they picked up a load of the newly-arrived slaves. During that night the tug went back up river and past Savannah. The load of slaves was put ashore at the plantation of John Montmollin.

Years later one of the men who claimed to have been an investor in the *Wanderer*, A.C. McGhee, related a story that found its way into print. These statements were made by Mr. McGhee when he was an old man and appear to be inaccurate due to his poor memory of events that had happened many years before. He stated that Lamar was able to sneak the slave-laden *Wanderer* up the river past Savannah and the Federal fort by holding some sort of dinner party and dance that distracted the guardians of the river. In fact, the *Wanderer* never did go up the river, according to Henderson's *The Slave Ship* Wanderer, and if there is any truth to McGhee's story it is quite possible that he was thinking of the steam tug *Lamar*. True or not, the story of the *Wanderer*'s trip up the river lives on in print, and the reports of that night do not seem out of character for the bold blockade runner.

The newly-landed slaves spoke no English and were easily identified by their ability to mimic various phrases in different languages as well as by their filed teeth and tattoos. They stood out so much wherever they showed up in public that rumors were soon circulating that a new load of slaves had been landed, widely believed to from the *Wanderer*. Sightings of these "greenies" by various members of the public confirmed suspicions that some ship had recently run the blockade.

Freshly cleaned, *Wanderer* was moved to Brunswick, Georgia, where she received clearance after a quick look at her incomplete papers by Collector Woodford Mabry. Not long after clearing her, Mabry had second thoughts that *Wanderer* may have been the slaver that was increasingly rumored. He returned, and this time he went aboard to inspect her first hand. Although she was clean and looked legitimate, closer inspection proved that the fittings for the temporary decking had not been completely removed, along with other signs of her illicit activity. With the proof he needed in hand, Mabry immediately canceled her clearance. When the steam tug *Lamar* showed up to move *Wanderer* to Savannah, Mabry would not allow her to be moved. Alarmed, Corrie abandoned his "yacht" and left charts, letters, papers, and even his trunk aboard.

The truth was out, and it was not limited to the area around Savannah. On December 16, 1858 the United States Senate passed a resolution asking the President to communicate any information available "in relation to the landing of the barque *Wanderer* on the coast of Georgia with a cargo of Africans."

In February of 1859 United States District Judge John Nicoll (who was also Charles Lamar's father-in-law) decreed that the *Wanderer* was forfeit to the United States and would be sold at auction. In mid-March an auction was held, attended by Lamar and his friends. One friend announced that the ship rightfully belonged to Lamar and stated that anybody bidding on the vessel would be punched. Only two bids were made: a jailer named Charles Van Horn bid $4,000, and Charles Lamar bid $4,001, which was quickly accepted. Just at that time, Lamar slugged Van Horn, putting an end to further bidding. The yacht and all gear aboard was returned to Lamar, but his legal troubles were not over. On May 28, 1860, a trial against Lamar was held for violation of slave-trade laws. When the judge warned the prosecution that the testimony given had failed to link Lamar directly with the yacht, the prosecution moved for permission not to prosecute, and all charges were dropped. The legal establishment in Savannah was not strongly in favor of supporting Yankee anti-slave trade laws, especially against powerful native sons and even more especially the one married to the judge's daughter.

While awaiting trial, Lamar was also trying to sell the *Wanderer*. Extensive refurbishing was required to make her saleable, and her reputation as a slaver had vastly decreased her value as a pleasure craft. Lamar even took her to Havana to look for buyers interested in running slaves to Cuba. When a man named David Martin offered $20,000 for a three-quarter interest in her, Lamar was ready to sell. Martin claimed that he wanted to go into the "fruit importation" business and thus needed a fast boat. A major problem was that Martin did not have anywhere near enough money to complete the purchase. To keep the boat from sailing prior to his receiving full payment, Lamar had stored some of her equipment in a warehouse. Martin bribed or otherwise talked a watchman at Lamar's warehouse into letting him take some of the sails and gear out of the warehouse and put them on the boat. Upon learning this, the angered Lamar had the vessel moved away from the dock and had his clerk demand immediate payment of the balance due from Martin. Lamar then left town on legal business, but when he returned to Savannah he spotted the yacht at anchor. He was told that a crew was being formed and supplies had been brought aboard the ship. Lamar sought help from Customs Collector John Boston, who advised Lamar that since the revenue cutter was out of port and since he had no way to reach the *Wanderer*, nothing could be done to stop her that day. It is unclear why Lamar didn't put a steam tug or one of his other vessels at Boston's disposal. The next morning, when dawn broke and visibility grew, it became apparent that *Wanderer* was gone from her mid-river mooring. News quickly came in that she was aground down river. Lamar followed on a steam tug, but the tide had lifted *Wanderer* off of the sand bar, and she had sailed away on a journey that would allow her to live up to her name.

The tale of *Wanderer's* ensuing adventures was about as bizarre a pirate's yarn as they come. A drunken captain had forced crew members to sign on under threat of a pistol and then had sailed the ship away with no charts or navigation books, few supplies, and a rapidly dwindling supply of liquor. Amazingly, this ragtag bunch of pirates managed to make it all the way to the Azores, where they somehow got re-supplied. In their haste to depart those Portuguese islands they left the ship's carpenter behind. There were two very good reasons for their haste. They hadn't paid for the supplies, and on-board they had two young Portuguese or Azorean girls that Martin later stated he would trade for slaves in Africa. First mate Henry Wilton wanted nothing to do with kidnapping and slaving, although he had to have been aware of the original intent of the voyage, and upon arrival at Madeira he joined with the second mate to plan the ship's salvation.

Because a man-of-war was seen in the harbor at Madeira, Martin didn't enter that port, but instead he headed the ship down the African coast with plans to stop vessels and take provisions by force. When a vessel voluntarily agreed to provide provisions, Martin went with some of his men in a small boat to pick them up. On board *Wanderer*, which had been hastily renamed William, first mate Wilton took command, telling the crew of his intention to give up the ship to American authorities. The crew agreed, and Capt. Martin was left somehow to find his way back to America— which he eventually did, through Liverpool, England.

On Christmas Eve of 1859, Wilton and his crew sailed *Wanderer* into Boston harbor, where they turned her over to customs. The crew claimed they had been hired on to import fruit from Cuba, but the court refused to believe them and in fact ended up condemning the vessel as a slave runner. Charles Lamar's father, Gazaway, claimed ownership and appealed the condemnation. She was free from Federal custody for a short time, but a week before the Civil War broke out the *Wanderer* showed up in Key West and the United States Navy recaptured her. The justification used for that capture was the claim that she would make too fine blockade runner if she were allowed to remain free. Based on her history up until that time, they were quite correct and with the political situation degrading rapidly, the Navy felt free to act without great concern for immediate legal resolution of ownership questions. The ship's immediate potential use in support of the impending Union war effort was of much greater importance than paper ownership, which would clearly take years to be resolved.

After making his way back to Liverpool, the abandoned Martin attempted and almost pulled off a similar ship hijack, but he was uncovered and subsequently shipped back to the United States as a destitute seaman. Upon arrival he was arrested in November, 1860. In a wonderfully ironic twist of fate, due to the start of the Civil War, the case against him was held in a Confederate States

Court under the case title of *The United States v. David S. Martin*. Confederate District Judge Nicoll presided (still Charles Lamar's father-in-law). Martin, not surprisingly, was found guilty and sent away for five years.

In June of 1862 the United States court finalized its finding to condemn *Wanderer* for slave running activities. Because she had those large water tanks for the slave trade, her principal use by the Union Navy was to replenish the water supplies of blockade steamers on patrol. At the end of the Civil War she was sold at auction in Key West.

In March of 1865, Mary Chesnut recorded in her diary that she had seen "the sister of Captain Corrie, the anachronism who tried in the 19th century to reopen the African slave trade. He was the captain of the *Wanderer*, which was wrecked when she tried to land her black cargo." In spite of Mrs. Chesnut's error about the true fate of the ship, Mary Chesnut's comment indicates the notoriety that the Wanderer and her captain had achieved.

As soon as possible after the outbreak of war, Charles Lamar's father Gazaway B. Lamar returned to Georgia from New York and took charge of his business affairs. Charles went into the service of the Confederacy. He organized and was Lieutenant Colonel of the 7th Georgia Battalion. Upon the merging of 7th Georgia with the 61st Georgia Infantry, Charles was "thrown out by what he considers unjust treatment." Until late in the war he worked in a variety of business and blockade-running ventures with his father and acted as agent for the state of Georgia.

11

CHARLES AUGUSTUS LAFAYETTE LAMAR:

A Stronger Blockade

The Union blockade of the Southern States was initially ineffective, but over it time was very successful in causing increasingly severe shortages of a wide variety of supplies across the South. The huge profits blockade runners made early in the war as they ran virtually unmolested into sparsely guarded ports had attracted C. A.L. and his father to start a blockade-running company. Since both father and son had long owned interests in ships, and since Charles had owned ships that ran the slave blockade, it was natural for them to get involved in blockade running with commercial cargo goods. Both men owned substantial quantities of cotton, and the blockade had made the European trade in that commodity extremely lucrative Not only was there profit to be made by sending their cotton to Europe and bringing goods in short supply back into the South, but it was also a move in support of the Confederate cause.

This was the logic behind the founding of the Importing and Exporting Company of Georgia. Ten men in total set up the company, including C.A.L. Lamar. It was to be run by Gazaway B. Lamar along with C.A.L. Lamar, aided by a board of directors. Not long after the initial announcement of the formation of the company, several million dollars had been raised and soon the subscription books were closed as all the stock had been sold. Good ships were in very short supply and very expensive in the Confederate States, so Charles A.L. Lamar was sent to Europe to buy one or more fast and capacious steamers for the new company, with Capt. Henry Hartstein as his technical advisor.

Demand in the South and in England for capable blockade-running ships had quickly driven up their prices. As Charles Lamar searched for investors in England, Hartstein's sudden death struck left him without critical technical advice, but soon Lamar's friend and relative Captain John N. Maffitt was recruited to take the post. Maffitt was himself well-known as the captain of the Confederate commerce raider *Florida*, and later in the war he would command blockade runners owned by the Confederate government. Maffitt went on to become one of the last blockade runners of the war when he ran the fast steamer *Owl* into Galveston in the spring of 1865.

Charles' hard work was finally rewarded when he cut a business deal with a Liverpool merchant Henry Lafone that he and his father had other dealings with. An agreement was made to acquire the *Lilian*, and subsequent dealings resulted in the purchase of partial interests in four other steamers. Negotiations by another agent resulted in another two boats. Unfortunately, one problem after another frustrated the best attempts of the company to make a profit. The wreck of the blockade runner *Ceres* as C.A.L. Lamar was returning to the South aboard her the offered an indication of things to come.

Ironically, it was the laws of the Confederacy that were to cause the Importing and Exporting Company of Georgia some of its greatest headaches. The Confederate Congress passed a bill in February 1864 allowing the President of the Confederacy to regulate blockade runners. Jefferson Davis decreed in March of 1864 that one half of all cargo space on privately owned vessels had to be reserved for Confederate cargo, and shippers' profits fell as their cargoes were effectively halved. By the end of 1864 the company was $100,000 in debt, and its stock was worthless. At the same time, Sherman was marching through Georgia, and the advance of Union forces soon halted all remaining operations.

Charles A.L. Lamar re-entered the service of the Confederacy and was serving on the staff of General Howell Cobb in the final days of the war. His father had made the decision that continued resistance to an overwhelming and soon-to-be victorious force was futile. In order to retain his property he was willing to take an oath to support the Constitution of the United States, as had been proclaimed by President Lincoln in December 1863. After Charles' father Gazaway took the oath, he sent a letter to Charles that had been forwarded through the Union lines. Gazaway Bugg Lamar explained to his son the reasoning behind that decision, and suggested that Charles do the same. Always the firebrand, C. A.L. Lamar rejected the plea from his father that he should take the oath. His hard-line resistance was to cost Charles a lot more than just his monetary fortune. In a skirmish near Columbus with Union forces under General J. H. Wilson, Colonel Charles Augustus Lafayette Lamar, C.S.A., was shot dead, reportedly leading a skirmish charge. (Cate, L.Q.C. Lamar's biographer, states that C.A.L. Lamar had "come home to die in a gallant charge at Columbus, Georgia"). The date was April 16, 1865. General Robert E. Lee had surrendered four days earlier at Appomattox Court House. The *Savannah Morning News* referred to Charles as "the last man who fell in the organized struggle for Southern independence."

In an interesting twist of history, years after Charles died, a worker at a Northern paper mill happened to take a close look at a package of documents ready to be loaded into the machinery to be pulped. The worker, a student at a summer job, found something of interest that caught his eye. It was a packet of papers that turned out to be C.A.L. Lamar's correspondence, recording much that had gone on in the days before the start of the war and detailing Charles' actions as he put together his investment groups to buy slave-trading blockade runners. These papers were published in the *North American Review* in November of 1886, thus insuring that Charles A.L. Lamar's activities have been footnoted and documented in most of the books written on the subject of slavery since that time.

The author of the *North American Review* article is not named, since the article was published in the No Name Series, but the author was a high school or college student. In his introduction to the article he states

> It was my fortune, during my summer's vacation, to rescue from the obliterating maw of a New England paper mill, a letter-press copy book, containing impressions of a series of remarkable letters, written by a prominent 'Southern Gentleman' of the 'days before the war'. Happening to glance over the contents of the book, I saw it had once been the property of Mr. C. A.L. Lamar, of Savannah, Georgia, a cousin, I believe, of Hon. L.Q.C. Lamar, our present United States Secretary of Interior. It must have been confiscated during 'Sherman's March to the Sea" and brought North. It fell, I suppose, into unappreciative hands, or else it would have been utilized before this time, and not so carelessly doomed to destruction.

Other letters written by Lamar show that he was actively interested in banking schemes, horse breeding enterprises, turf affairs, and many sorts of business, but all of them rigidly consistent with Southern "gentility" and "chivalry." When he entered into the slave trade, he made no apologies for it. He was a man claiming such high honor that he would permit no question of his actions, but he repeatedly offered to demonstrate his ethics by standing up at five or ten paces and drawing his conclusions from his skill with pistols.

The red headed firebrand's intentions are made clear in the following letter, written in June of 1860 to L.Q.C. Lamar:

> Dear Lucius;
> I wrote you sometime during the winter, requesting you to telegraph me when Raymond of the New York Times arrived in Washington, that I might go and meet him. You

never replied, and I therefore feel some hesitancy in again addressing you; but I'll try it once more. I received the enclosed through the mail this morning, and being unable to decipher the name of Mr. C who franked it, though I sent to the Post Office and made the request to them to give me the name, I send it to you, with the request that you will find out who sent it to me, and demand of him, in my name, if he intended in anyway to reflect on me by addressing it "In Jail." If he did, challenge him peremptorily in my name and telegraph me, and I will be there to meet the appointment. I am not in jail . . . If I go out on the field, the result will be a very different one from the one I had with Commodore Moore, against whom I had no feeling. If you feel any hesitancy in acting in accordance with the within, turn it over to my friend, Jack Jones. He will do the needful. I am very truly yours, etc. C.A.L. Lamar

We are left to wonder in this subject ever came up between the two cousins aboard the *Ceres* as they crossed from Bermuda on their way home from Europe to the doomed Confederacy to whose principles they both gave so much.

12

MIRABEAU BUONAPARTE LAMAR:

The Georgia Years

Mirabeau Buonaparte Lamar, later to become a famous Texas hero, was born in 1798 near Louisville, Georgia, which was then the state capital. He was the son of John and Rebecca Lamar. By the early 1800s John had moved the family to a location eight miles south of the town of Eatonton, in Putnam County, Georgia, to a large plantation named Fairfield on the banks of the Little John River. An indication of the original size of the plantation may be gathered from Cate's comment in his 1935 book on L.Q.C. Lamar. Cate stated that the homestead had passed into the hands of the Georgia Power Company, and that "today almost one thousand acres remain about the house."

Here John lies buried, under a headstone authored by his son Mirabeau that tells us much of what we know about the hero's father:

> In memory of John Lamar, who died August 3, 1833, aged
> sixty-four years. He was a man of unblemished honor, of
> pure and exalted benevolence, whose conduct through life
> was uniformly regulated by the strictest principles of pro-
> bity, truth and justice: thus leaving behind him as the best
> legacy to his children a noble example of constant virtue. In
> his domestic relations he was greatly blessed, receiving from

> every member of a large family unremitting demonstrations
> of respect, love and obedience.

John, reported to be a man of culture and wealth, had married his first cousin, Rebecca Lamar. Their other children were Lucius Quintus Cincinnatus (father of the future Supreme Court Justice), Jefferson Jackson, Thomas Randolph, and five daughters. In those days, marriage between cousins was more accepted than it is today, perhaps due both to a lack of knowledge of potential problems as well as to the limited number of eligible candidates.

W. H. Sparks grew up with Mirabeau Buonaparte Lamar, and in his book titled *The Memories of Fifty Years*, published in 1882, he describes the young man:

> There was in him a natural chivalry of character, which
> characterized him above all of his early compeers [*sic*], and
> made him a model in conduct. He received his education
> principally at Milledgeville and at Putnam. From his earliest
> boyhood he was remarkable for his genius and great moral
> purity. His ardent, practical temperament was accompanied
> with exquisite modesty, and a gentle playfulness of disposi-
> tion: with an open unaffected kindness of heart, which as a
> boy rendered him popular with his fellows at school, and
> beloved by his teachers. . . .

In 1819 after completing his education, the 22-year-old Mirabeau B. Lamar moved to Alabama to open a general store in Cahawba. His partner, Willis Roberts, had been a friend of his father, and Cahawba was their choice because the state, newly admitted to the Union, had picked that river-front location as the site of the new state's capitol. Mirabeau soon found that running a store was not to his liking, so he sold his interest and bought one-half interest in the *Cahawba Press*, one of two weekly newspapers in town. When the newspaper failed to thrive, Lamar returned to Georgia, where his initiation into political life came when he was appointed to the position of "confidential clerk" to Georgia Governor George Troup. The elder Lucius Q. C. Lamar's law partner, Joel Crawford, had been involved with Troup's campaign and was helpful in getting Mirabeau this job. In March of 1825, the Governor invited Mirabeau to travel to Savannah to help in the reception of an honored hero of the American Revolution, the aged General Marquis de Lafayette. The United States Congress had in 1824 passed a resolution inviting Lafayette to visit as a guest of the nation. It was well known that the much-beloved Frenchman had spent heavily from his own pocket to support the American Revolution, and having lost most of his property during the French Revolution, he was deeply in debt at the time of the invitation from Congress. Vincent Nolte, in *Memoirs of a Merchant*, quotes Lafayette at that time as saying that "I have here in Paris debts to the amount of 100,000 francs which must be repaid before I dare go to another quarter of the world. I could procure the money here, if I would give a mortgage on my estate of LaGrange, but it is the heritage of my children—it belonged to my wife, and now is theirs."

In order to permit the aged war hero to leave France these debts were paid be three people: James Brown, United States Minister to France; an unidentified Dutchman; and Jean Girod of New Orleans. Lafayette departed France in the company of his son George Washington Lafayette and arrived in New York almost forty years after he had last departed. He was received in New York on a grand scale, and followed with a tour of New England, where he was similarly received. Aging veterans of the Revolution waited for hours to greet Lafayette as his party moved along the old Post Road on his way to Boston. From New England the tour went on to Washington, where a grateful United States Congress in December of 1824 voted Lafayette a grant of $200,000 and a township of 24,000 acres in Florida. This French hero of the revolution was no longer under any financial pressure, and with this generous gift of Congress he was in fact quite well off. Concluding an extended stay in the nation's capital, Lafayette then visited the site of the final battlefield of the Revolution at Yorktown, Virginia.

From there Lafayette went to spend a week at Monticello with Thomas Jefferson before turning even further south toward Savannah, where on March 19 Mirabeau Lamar greeted Lafayette as an official emissary of the state of Georgia. Mirabeau was leading a corps of troops which escorted Lafayette not only during his three-day stay in that city, but on to Augusta aboard the steamboat *Altamaha*. Later, after proper festivities in Augusta, they went to the state capitol. Lamar also escorted and guided the General on a tour of the Creek Nation in Georgia.

The remainder of Lafayette's grand and final American tour took him on to New Orleans and then up the Mississippi by boat. Finally, the grand tour got back on land and set out across the country to return in June to Boston, where Lafayette laid the cornerstone of the Bunker Hill Memorial before progressing again to Washington. There President John Quincy Adams was able to convince Lafayette to stay in the White House. Festivities continued, and the newly built frigate *Brandywine* was made ready to carry the hero home to France. Virtually every city, town and hamlet that had been visited had showered gifts upon him, so when he departed, the ship had a cargo of gifts that included Indian artifacts, stuffed and live animals, models of steam engines, furniture, and a seemingly endless and varied list of other items. He had visited all twenty-six states that then made up the initial United States. The country that he had helped to bring into existence had richly thanked him for his generous support in earlier times and insured that his final years would be without financial want or concern.

On New Year's Day of the year following Lafayette's visit, Mirabeau B. Lamar married Tabitha B. Jordan at her family's home city of Perry, Alabama. After Governor Troup lost his re-election bid, the Lamars set out for the newly laid-out city of Columbus, Georgia, where M. B. Lamar founded the *Columbus Enquirer* in May of 1828. Many of the newspapers in those days were political, and Lamar stated in the paper's broadside prospectus that

Under the above title the subscriber proposes to publish a
Newspaper in the town of Columbus if sufficient patronage can be obtained to warrant the undertaking . . .
The Columbus Enquirer will be attached to the Republican creed as exemplified in the administration of Thomas
Jefferson; and in state politics, adhering to the principles
that characterized the late able administration of Governor
Troup, it will defend 'the union of the States and the sover-
eignty of the States'
TERMS-THE ENQUIRER will be printed on a large sheet,
with new type, once a week, at THREE DOLLARS, per
ann. in advance of four dollars at the end of the year.

Sufficient patronage was obtained not only to launch the paper
but to sustain it up to the present day.

M. B. Lamar's first run for public office came in 1829, when
he was elected to the state legislature. Either for financial purposes
or to have more time to travel on political business, he sold one-
half of the newspaper.

But while his political life was prospering, personal tragedy
was about to strike. His wife, unfortunately, was not a strong
woman, and she lived only long enough to bear a daughter. After
his wife's death from tuberculosis, Mirabeau, finding himself in
poor health and poor spirits, arranged for the care of his daughter
with relatives in Georgia, and went on an extended trip or trips.
Returning to Georgia in 1832, he announced that he would be a
candidate for the United States House of Representatives, but he
failed to gain the nomination of his chosen party. Running as an
independent, he was badly beaten. That must have been a time in
his life when he felt the need for a new challenge in a new place.

13

MIRABEAU BUONAPARTE LAMAR:

Instant Hero, then President

By 1834 Mirabeau had sold his remaining interest in the *Enquirer* and was ready to move on. Many Georgians at that time were attracted to the new lands in Texas. One of them was Lamar's friend James W. Fannin, who later led a mostly-Georgian troop in the battle for Texas independence. Seeking new lands and new challenges, Lamar was also attracted by Texas, and there he journeyed in 1835. Having made the decision to emigrate to and settle in Texas, Lamar told several people including Stephen Austin, whom he soon met, about his conviction. He told Austin that the first thing he had to do was to return temporarily to Georgia to settle his business affairs.

After completing his business in Georgia, in April of 1836 Lamar returned by ship to Texas. Upon landing at Velasco he learned that there was serious trouble with Mexico. Lamar had brought with him $6000 from some Georgian investors to buy land, so his first task was to find a safe place for cash. An individual was needed, since banks either did not exist or were not to be trusted. For this delicate responsibility, Lamar chose the second in command of the Provisional Government, Vice-President de Zevala. Later, when it came time to collect the cash, the decision proved to have been a good one, and Lamar learned first-hand that Zevala was an honest man.

The previous October, when Mexican troops had attempted

to retrieve a cannon that they had loaned to Texans for use against Indian attacks, the Texans unfurled a battle flag that said "COME AND TAKE IT." The attempt to take it set off a round of reactions and skirmishes. Events moved rapidly, and the Mexican leader, General Santa Ana marched a strong force into Texas. By March of 1836, while Lamar had been back in Georgia selling off property, Santa Ana had attacked and overrun the Alamo. Lamar had therefore not been among the Alamo defenders, nor had he returned to Texas in time to be at Goliad where almost all the captured Texans—including his friend Fannin—were slaughtered along the roadside after being promised their repatriation to the United States.

Upon his return to Texas it was clear to Mirabeau Lamar that he was in the middle of a violent storm. In a letter to his brother Jefferson Jackson Lamar dated April 10, 1836, Mirabeau Buonaparte Lamar wrote

> I leave this morning for the Army, a dreadful battle is to be fought in three or four days on the Brazos, decisive of the fate of Texas; I shall of course have to be in it. William D. Redd of Columbus is with me. Texas is in a dreadful state of confusion; the Mexicans thus far are prevailing. St antonio(sic) has been retaken by them and every man in the fort murdered. Crocket was among the number. Fanin's army is entirely destroyed. After fighting four or five hours, the enemy held out the white flag and proposed terms of capitulation to which Fannin yielded. The terms of surrender was that they were all to be transported to New Orleans, not again to engage in the War; they were about four hundred, including Ward's men, and Capt. Millers first arrived & taken at Copano. They were kept prisoners 9 days, then marched out and fired upon & all butchered with the exception of two or three who escaped by flight. Almost the whole of Americans from Georgia and Alabama have perished.
>
> The amount placed in Zavalo's hands is six thousand dol-

lars; Redd, the President, D. G. Burnet, Potter and others saw me give the money to him, and can be evidence of the fact if I should lose the receipt. I hope the gentleman for whom I am acting will believe that I have acted for the best . . . I am confident they will acquit me of any selfish disregard of their interest.

My health at present is good. I feel much solitude for my mother; If she was well and cheerful & could bear affliction with more fortitude I should be happy—Tell Rebecca Ann that she must learn to read and write & spell well, and that is the best education—I have petitioned to the Govt. for my League of Land as a citizen of Texas in 1835; but the Gvt. will do nothing on it; I think however the testimony of Hoxey and Christman the surveyor of my intention to return to the country as a citizen will hereafter secure the land when the war is over.

Mirabeau Lamar also mentioned in that letter that he had written an informal will, which was stored with his papers and other belongings. The tone and character of the letter are clearly one of a man heading off to a do-or-die struggle. On March 25, Alexander Patton of Velasco wrote to a man named Kilgore from Brazoria, asking that the horse that was being kept for him be given to M. B. Lamar. This may have been the horse that Lamar finally ended up with, since various reports say that he entered the battle on a "borrowed" horse. Luckily, Lamar caught up with Houston's army near Hempstead and enlisted in Houston's growing but rag-tag army of about 800, most of whom were settlers and frontiersmen.

San Jacinto was the place that Sam Houston had chosen to take his stand after repeatedly evading Santa Ana's superior force. Water, in the form of Buffalo Bayou and the San Jacinto River (really more of a creek) and marshes enclosed three sides of the battlefield. Buffalo Bayou was deep, and although narrow, at that time it was full of water right up to the top of the banks. An artillery duel with Santa Ana's troops had prompted the Texans to pull back into the cover of a grove of live oak trees. Two cannons, nicknamed the "Two Sisters," had just been received from supporters in the United States, and although the Texans had not had the time to sight them in, one of the first rounds was lucky enough to knock out a Mexican field piece. Perhaps this lucky shot was an indication of things to come.

Not long after arriving, Lamar went to Houston with the plan to enlist 300 volunteers and go aboard the riverboat *Yellowstone* for the purpose of raiding behind the enemy lines. Houston responded in part by posting a public warning that any person who "beat for volunteers" would be considered a traitor and would be shot. Apparently having heard the message loud and clear, Lamar immediately threw his lot in with the cavalry as a private. One day before the actual start of the battle, a firefight broke out during a cavalry probe of the enemy lines. Thomas Jefferson Rusk, Texas' Secretary of War, was surrounded by Mexican dragoons and was in immediate danger of capture or death. Mirabeau Buonaparte Lamar, astride a big stallion and brandishing his distinctive curved saber, charged one of the Mexican horseman, knocked down his horse, and opened up a path that allowed Rusk to escape. Moments later, while heading back to his own battle lines, Lamar came upon a 19-year-old Texan named Walter Lane who had been knocked from his horse and was about to be killed by a mounted Mexican. Lamar charged in with his pistol blazing, killed the Mexican and saved Lane's life, and they both escaped back to the Texas lines. (Lane later went on to become a General in the Civil War). Folklore has it that the Mexicans were so impressed by Lamar's exploits and horsemanship during that skirmish that they applauded him right there on the field of battle, applause that he is said to have acknowledged with a bow.

Sam Houston quickly became aware of these heroic acts, which came at a time when bold and successful moves were badly needed. Houston acted quickly and virtually on the spot Private Lamar became Colonel Lamar. It would seem logical that this promotion had the backing of the Texan Secretary of War, whose life had just been saved by the promotee. At the time of the promotion Houston initially discussed having Lamar take over the artillery corps, but Lamar declined, saying that they were doing a fine job and he didn't want to steal their glory. He told Houston that he preferred to remain a private in the cavalry. The cavalry troops then asked Lamar to head their unit, which he immediately accepted. Since the former cavalry head was one of those who requested that Lamar lead them, there was no ill will about the abrupt change.

The next day Houston held a council of war, and the volunteer army, sick of continually retreating from Santa Ana, rejected Houston's plan to wait yet another day for the attack. Ready to fight, the army voted to strike immediately, and Houston swung into action. He started by sending his best scout, "Deaf" Smith to cut off Santa Ana's only potential means of retreat, Vince's Bridge. It was late in the afternoon when the battle finally got underway. Santa Ana had anticipated an attack that morning, but when the morning passed to afternoon without an attack, he ordered his men to rest. The Mexican Generalissimo planned to attack the Texans that very next morning. That fateful afternoon Santa Ana is reputed to have chosen the company of a young woman, and, as the story goes, was somewhat preoccupied with her when the Texans opened fire. Although armies usually post pickets to give early warning of enemy movements, the Mexicans had been lax in this regard. The Texans, with their cannons—the "Two Sisters"—and with Mirabeau Buonaparte Lamar leading sixty cavalrymen, literally caught the Mexicans napping. Cries of "Remember Goliad" and "Remember The Alamo" urged the Texans on and thus they reminded themselves that sure death was the only alternative to total victory. Thus motivated, they overran the enemy's defensive perimeter, and the Mexicans quickly went from enjoying their siesta and preparing dinner to chaotic retreat. Almost immediately the Texans captured the Mexican cannons and turned them upon their former owners. About then, Santa Ana's army lost all discipline and their main camp was soon overrun and fell. No longer an army, they broke ranks and panicked as Texans rode through the remainder of their defenses and easily smashed down their camp. Mexican troops fled, and the Texans chased them into the swamps and tall grass. The whole shooting-match was over in less than a half an hour. The next day stragglers attempting to escape were being rounded up by a group of Texans on patrol when the patrol spotted a deer and attempted to shoot it. The deer fled, frightened by something in the tall grass and ran away in a direction that caused the hunters to suspect the presence of yet another Mexican in hiding. The hunters went to see what had frightened the deer, and there in the grass they found and captured General Santa Ana, who had attempted to hide his identity dressed as a private.

The battle had been won in an absolutely glorious fashion, and Texas was saved from Mexican control. The victors immediately became heroes of the struggle for Texas independence by the very fact that they had been in that victorious army. Several men in Houston's army became well known in Texas because of their exploits at this battle. "Deaf" Smith is remembered to this day and has a county named after him, as does Mirabeau Lamar.

Lamar's actions on the eve of the battle catapulted him from an unknown to a hard-riding troop leader with superb horsemanship who had engaged the enemy and performed heroically. Houston, in his official written report to the interim government, stated that "Our cavalry, sixty-one in number, commanded by Colonel Mirabeau B. Lamar, (whose gallant and daring conduct on the previous day had attracted the admiration of his comrades and called him to that station,) placed on our right, completed our line . . ."

The Texans had captured quite a supply of Mexican weapons, stores of food, and other goods, along with $12,000 in cash. Some of the captured goods were auctioned off, including Santa Ana's ornately-decorated saddle, which Lamar won with a bid of $300.

There was another man with the family name of Lamar involved in that famous battle, as well: Houston's battle report incorrectly lists him as Shelly W. Lamar, a private in Company B of the Volunteers. Not much is known about this second Lamar, and it is appears that he did not remain in Texas, since a letter dated February 11, 1838 in the Lamar papers of the Texas State Library, from Shelby W. Lamar, (clearly the same person) of Mt. Vernon, Illinois, reads in part "After parting with you at Irwinton I made the best of my way to this place and after verry long and fatiguing journey reached hear in safety. I have writing some two or three times . . ." He went on to give his personal regard for M. B. Lamar and inquired regarding legislation that had been pending when he left Texas that would give those in the service at the time of San Jacinto one-half a league of land.

Again in 1840 the same Shelby W. Lamar wrote to Mirabeau, again from Illinois: "After a long silence I again take the liberty of an old fellow soldier . . ." This somewhat flowery letter goes on to talk about Shelby Lamar's having married an amiable wife (who probably wrote or at least influenced the letter, an assumption this author has based on the vastly improved grammar and spelling), his two helpless children, his caring for an aging mother, and his poor health.

> Under these circumstances I am compelled to trespass upon one, whom I have known, only to revere and love. My heart, my hopes turn to you General, and the fertile plains of Texas where I fondly trust to recover my health and renew my usefulness. One, who lent his feeble aid to Texas in the hour of doubt and darkness would ask the privilege of earning his sustenance in her service in the day of her prosperity.
>
> I would immediately start with my family, but adequate means are wanting; and I earnestly solicit from you, General, an advance of funds sufficient for the present emergency, to bear me to a land where I may reap the fruits of my daily toil, and rest at eve under the protecting shadow of that glorious tree, which I assisted to plant on the plains of San Jacinto . . .

It is doubtful that Mirabeau Lamar ever advanced the money, since no thank you letter or other evidence of any debt (or in fact any other letter from Shelby) exists in the very extensive Lamar records. Another Lamar, John T. Lamar of Georgia, fought in the Texas Army at that time, but was not at the battle of San Jacinto. In June of 1839 he was back in Georgia, and commented in a letter to Mirabeau "Although I may never return to Texas . . ." Years later, in October of 1856, one John Frick of Philadelphia wrote concerning John Lamar's bounty claim for services in the Texas Army of 1836.

Following the battle of San Jacinto, Houston, who had been wounded in the ankle during that battle, had to travel out of Texas for medical attention. Rusk was appointed as the Head of the Army during the interim, and Lamar continued his rapid rise in the Texas government when he was appointed to replace Rusk as Secretary of War. The decision had been made by Houston and the Provisional Government to spare the life of Santa Ana, arguing that a live Santa Ana was a much more valuable bargaining chip than a dead one. Many of the troops, with painful memories of their friends who had been brutally killed at the Alamo and Goliad, wanted Santa Ana dead. Lamar didn't trust Santa Ana, but went along with the majority and backed the government's position. Of Santa Ana's promises to help Texas gain a peace treaty that would grant independence from Mexico, Lamar said these promises were "lighter than moonshine's watery beam. I trust them as I would a dicer's oath." The Interim President of Texas, David Burnet, removed Thomas Jefferson Rusk as Head of the Army because of the former's vocal and active advocacy of the position that Santa Ana should be hung. Chosen to replace him was his boss, Secretary of War M. B. Lamar. On June 25, 1836, Interim President Burnet proclaimed that "Be it known that reposing perfect trust and confidence in the Honor, patriotism, fidelity, and Ability of Mirabeau Buonaparte Lamar, I have nominated and by and with the advice and consent of my Cabinet, in virtue of the Authority vested in me do constitute and Appoint the said Mirabeau Buonaparte Lamar to the land and Office of Major General in the Army and Commander in Chief of all the forces in the service of Texas . . . "

In spite of the grand proclamation, the feelings among the troops ran high about the issue of Santa Ana, and following much agitation by their officers, the troops made it clear that they favored Rusk to lead them. When Lamar went to take command, the officers and men openly refused his command. They initially held a meeting and drafted resolutions as follows:

> Resolved—That this meeting highly appreciate the gallantry and worth of General Lamar, and will be at all times ready to receive him with the cordiality and respect due his personal and military acquirements.

> Resolved— . . . appointed a committee to wait on General Lamar, and tender him the respects of this meeting, and inform him that, there being some question of the propriety of his appointment by the President as major-general of the Texan Army, by which he is directed to assume the chief command of the army, he is requested by the officers present not to act in his official capacity of major-general until the subject may be more maturely considered by the meeting of the officers of the army.

Lamar was unwilling to accept the resolution but told them that he wished the opportunity to address the troops, which was arranged. He talked to the assembled troops about San Jacinto, and told them that he was not anxious to lead them if they didn't want him, but he would cheerfully join their ranks. Other officers spoke, and a vote was taken that went heavily against Lamar. In a letter to Burnet, Lamar wrote "I had an open rupture with General Rusk believing it to be the secret arrangmts of his to supplant me." Based on the outcome of the vote, Rusk stayed on, and the Army then called for the arrest of Burnet and the invasion of Mexico. The interim government was just that, and in increasing trouble.

When that interim government had been initially established, part of the agreement called for a Presidential election to be held in September of 1836. In June of that year, Burnet announced that the election would be held the first Monday of September. Houston was the Presidential candidate, and Mirabeau Buonaparte Lamar was put up for Vice-President. Those heroes of San Jacinto were, not surprisingly, both elected. Although he had first entered Texas the year before, because of his trip home to Georgia, Lamar had amazingly enough really only been in his new country a total of six months at the time of his election!

In spite of his rapidly growing reputation and fame, the pronunciation of his name was to be a recurring problem for the rough-and-ready settlers of Texas, who often referred to him as "Mee-ry-boo." During Houston's term as President, which was limited to one term by law, Lamar chafed under him and liked him less and less as the term went on. The dislike was mutual with the result that Houston, although unable to run against Lamar himself, supported first one then another candidate to run against Lamar for President. The campaign raised some small gossip such as the fact that the Vice-President had been indicted for drunkenness, but the talk did little harm since the charge had been dropped. (It is also hard to believe that even if he had been convicted that this would have been much of a problem to the hard-drinking Texans.) Sam Houston may not have been convicted of the same offense but was often reported to be under the influence of the Demon Rum, and the voters certainly had not found that to be a reason to vote against Houston. Widower Lamar was also taken to task for his involvement with Olivia Roberts, a friend from Georgia, who had followed him to Texas in 1837. Mirabeau was luckier than his opponents, since this also failed to evolve into a major problem. In a very strange set of circumstances, first one, then the second of the two candidates that Houston pushed to compete for the office committed suicide, leaving Lamar's election to be contested only by a self-nominated unknown named Bob Wilson. The opposition then brought up the question of Lamar's eligibility, specifi-

cally concerning his absence from Texas at the time that the Constitution had been adopted. To be elected, the law required that
the person had to have been a resident of Texas at the time the
Constitution took effect, or for three years prior to the date of the
election. In a letter dated June 16, 1838, answering one from
Samuel Whiting and J.W. Miles that raised the question of his
eligibility, Lamar wrote

> I beg leave to begin by stating that I came into this country
> in the month of July 1835, and have continued here from
> that date up to the present period, with the exception of
> two visits to my native state, on private business which
> could not without great injury to myself be longer delayed
> or neglected.
>
> I arrived at Nacogdoches at the date above specified, and
> proceeded thence to Coles' Settlement, where I made known
> to many gentlemen of the first standing in the Community,
> my determination to become a citizen of Texas; and in accor-
> dance with this determination paid Capt. Chrisman a law-
> ful surveyor of the Colony, a fee of forty or fifty dollars to
> run off my head right lands; the receipt for which I hold at
> the present moment. Besides this I made a public declara-
> tion before the people in their primary assembly at Wash-
> ington (on Brazos) when the war question was first agitated,
> that this country was not only to be my future home, but
> that I was resolved in the event of a revolutionary struggle,
> to make her destiny mine for good or ill . . .
>
> From Washington I came to San Felippe. The Land office
> was closed before I had an opportunity of procuring an
> order for my headright; but I was distinctly told by the
> Empresario, Col. Austin, that I could go to the United States,
> and return without forfeiting any of my rights by the visit.
> At Brazoria I reiterated my intention to settle in the coun-
> try—contributed my mite toward erecting a fort at
> Valesco . . .

Lamar's letter continued that he went to the United States, but hearing of trouble returned and "I landed at Valesco about the date of the massacre at Goliad. All was panic and confusion. The enemy was said to be close upon us. Unable to procure a horse, I started for our army on foot; and as a private soldier joined the ranks of the gallant few who were still holding out the banner of defiance to the foe. The battle of San Jacinto was fought and the country saved . . . "

Lamar goes on to cover his service to the country in the Cabinet as Attorney General and as Secretary of War, and then as Vice-President. The letter apparently resolved all meaningful questions, as he remained a candidate for election and was successful, with 6,995 votes to 252 for Wilson. Burnet, who had been the interim President before Houston, was elected Vice-President.

Houston, by now openly unfriendly to Lamar, had opposed his election on the basis that Lamar was a dreamer and a visionary lacking common sense. Houston, on the other hand, was known to spend a good deal of time removing the corks from whiskey bottles and had not proven to be a fiscal conservative. As the time for Lamar's inaugural approached, nobody seemed to know what the protocol should be regarding the newly minted ex-President. Someone suggested that the then former-President Houston give a brief speech, but Houston had plans of his own. Without having told anybody of these plans, he arrived at the platform dressed in Colonial costume, including a powdered wig, looking like George Washington. Towering over Lamar and most others on the platform, Houston took command of the podium and spoke for nearly three hours. Lamar was so clearly upset that he refused to give his own address and handed the speech to his secretary who read it in a flat monotone. Houston got the last laugh that day.

At the start of his term as the second President of the Republic of Texas (not counting, of course, the interim government), Lamar's country was suffering from an increasingly serious yellow fever outbreak and equally serious inflation caused by over a million dollars in poorly funded paper debt. This didn't keep him from ordering a new coach from New Orleans, complete with seal and flag, to be pulled by four horses, at the cost of the staggering sum of $2300. From his cousin Gazaway Bugg Lamar came congratulations on his election: "We have all seen with just admiration and delight your brilliant career in Texas. . . . We are proud of your success. . . . I hope your health will be so improved as to enable you to enjoy your well earned laurels, and that you may, unlike most modern heros, learn to wear them without ostentation and vain glory."

Prior to the start of his term in office, Lamar had joined some soldiers for a buffalo hunt not far from a fort on the Colorado River. At some point he went to the top of a hill and was very favorably impressed with the view, one that he did not forget. After becoming President he approved an act of the Texas Congress that called for a capital to be named after Stephen A. Austin and to be located between the Rivers Trinidad and Colorado, above the San Antonio Road. The commissioners that he appointed for the site selection were made aware of the hilltop site that he had visited and liked so much, and since it fell within the carefully worded geographic area, they picked the knoll for the location of Austin in spite of its being located on the edge of Indian territory. Some government buildings were quickly constructed, and the new President prepared to run the business of his new country from the site he had himself discovered some years earlier.

A week before he arrived at Austin, Indians had killed a group of thirteen people only a few miles outside of town. This may have been one of the factors that made putting an end to the "Indian Problem" a priority for the new president. This new state capital town was certainly at the edge of the frontier and must have looked like many a rough frontier settlement. For his office the President had a double log house on the corner of Congress and Eighth streets (in the usage of the time).

During his term in office and in his inaugural address Mirabeau Buonaparte Lamar opposed the annexation of Texas by the United States. He most likely believed that the United States was uninter-

ested in annexing Texas, and that may have influenced his thinking when he talked to the public concerning his thoughts of an
expanded Texas Republic. One problem that he accurately foresaw
was the potential problem relating to the undefined western boundaries of Texas. He foresaw the likelihood of problems with other
states if Texas were to join the Union. Another of his far-reaching
concerns was his anticipation of the need for a public school system. To provide for this he decreed that three leagues of land in
each county were to be set aside for primary schools, and that 50
leagues were to be surveyed and used to establish two colleges or
universities that would be created at some unspecified date in the
future. As it turned out, 40 years passed before these universities
came into existence, but they have become great institutions of
higher education.

A Homestead Act was enacted to protect settlers land against
foreclosure, a law that was needed to attract new settlers to this
country with an abundance of land and little else. If a settler were
to be hit with financial adversity due to crop failure or some other
reason, the pioneering homestead would not be lost to creditors.
Lamar also founded the Philosophical Society of Texas. In addition, he saw to it that provision was made for establishing a State
Library, something that certainly has made life easier for future
historians hoping to trace his efforts and actions. It was probably
because Lamar had been a newspaperman and had plans to write a
history of Texas that he appreciated the need for a good library.
The opposite side of this great man was that he took a very strong
stand against the Indians, taking for justification the legalistic position that they had not been given any rights under the Mexicans
or the earlier Texans. He considered any treaties that had been
entered into with Indians as not totally agreed to and certainly not
binding. Given these beliefs, it is not surprising that he was ruth-
less in attempting to drive the Indians out of Texan territory. His
expenditures in fighting the Indians were ten times what Houston
had spent on the same task during his first term in office. No one
can know what, if any, actions toward the Indians would have

brought peace, but due to Lamar's strong stand the Indians were often on the war path and eventually were driven out of much of their territory in Texas. Whereas Houston seemed to have been of the mind to buy them beads and engage in discussions, Lamar was of the mind to shoot first and ask questions later.

Descriptions of the man himself paint a picture of a person who some thought to be somewhat diffident unless and until a topic interested him, which would then bring out his spirit or alternately his wrath. He could be warm and witty with a limited number of his closest confidants around him, but he proved to be the opposite in large crowds. He had long been a poet and an author and the story is told that one time when he was visiting his friend Sam Goode of Alabama, Goode's daughter Emily asked Lamar to write something in her album. While picking up the pen he noticed that the preceding entry had been written by John Howard Payne, author of "Home Sweet Home," who had written in Emily's book:

> Lady, your name if understood
> Explains your nature to a letter
> And may you never change from Goode
> Unless if possible to better

When he finished reading the author's words, Lamar picked up the pen and immediately wrote

> I am content with being Goode
> To aim at better might be vain
> But if I do its understood
> Whate'er the cause it is no Payne.

While his treatment of the Indians was one dark episode of his time in office, perhaps the worst was the ill-fated Santa Fe expedition. The town of Santa Fe and the surrounding territory was at that time controlled by Mexico. There was widespread belief, at least among the Texans, that the settlers in Santa Fe wished to break away from the Mexicans and join Texas. In addition, there was a profitable trade over the Santa Fe Trail that was also of some appeal to Texans. A motion was put before the Texas Congress to fund an expedition to Santa Fe to "explore," but the motion was defeated. Not deterred, Lamar, still the bold leader and warrior, ordered the Comptroller in March of 1841 to open an account for the expedition and sent an agent to New Orleans to buy supplies. While there, the agent met a man named George Kendall. A native of New Hampshire, Kendall had worked for Horace Greeley and apparently had taken his advice to "Go West." He founded the institution that continues to this day as the *Picayune* newspaper in New Orleans. In spite of his newspaper success, Kendall was restless for adventure, and upon learning of the expedition, sought to join as an observer, paying his own way.

Back in Texas the expedition was mustering. A social gathering celebrating the forming of the group was held in San Antonio, and one Mary Maverick got the opportunity to record her observations of President Lamar. She noted that he wore wide, white pants which were short enough to show all of his shoe. The evening opened with a dance, and Lamar took as his partner Mrs. Juan Seguin, the wife of the mayor. Maverick noted that while he was a poet and brave, he was not the best dancer. Furthermore, his partner was fat, which made them a funny looking couple.

Arriving by ship, George Kendall traveled to San Antonio and caught up with the Expedition as the troops prepared to leave. The very night before the Expedition was to depart, while Kendall was attempting to walk to the river in the dark of night, he fell down an embankment and broke his leg in several places. President Lamar arranged to get him a Jersey wagon and two mules so he could continue the journey. This accident was but a taste of things to come.

When the whole expedition had traveled about twenty miles out of Austin, they camped and the President rode out to join them. It was reported that he unsaddled and staked his own horse, cooked his own meal, and spent the evening with the adventurers. The following day Lamar addressed them before he returned to Austin. This group of optimistic adventurers had no idea of what lay between them and Santa Fe. Nobody had ever crossed to Sante Fe from that part of Texas, at least not that anybody in the expedition knew of. That the trail was nonexistent was of no great concern to this optimistic group of adventure-seekers. The *Austin Sentinel* printed a highly unrealistic prediction that the journey would be 450 miles through "rich, rolling, well watered country." This piece of journalistic fluff reflected the dreams of the author and the hopes of the adventurous group, but both proved to be totally false. Before the trip was over the weary group was forced to dig roadways up and down steep river embankments, suffer prairie fire that consumed their wagons, endure severe thirst, and suffer death at the hands of Indians. They were lost for hundreds of miles, since they had only a longitude and latitude to go by, and the one guide who claimed to know the way had mistaken the Wichita River for the Red River. The so-called guide deceived them about his mistake for weeks before he finally deserted the group. The crowning blow, however, was the fact that the residents of Santa Fe, long aware of their progress, were fortified by a military force led by the Mexican Governor. The well-equipped, well-fed, and well-prepared Mexicans had no trouble at all with the survivors, who were more in need of rescue than anything even remotely resembling combat. The Mexicans saved them from near death and took them into captivity. Kendall, despite his protestations that he was an American observer and not a Texan, was also held until April of 1842. The expedition was an absolute and total disaster. If anything positive can be said about this ill-fated expedition, it is that Kendall's reporting did serve to increase the awareness in the United States of the Southwest and California, which were both still controlled by Mexico. Certainly that increase in public awareness was a far cry from the result that Lamar and his fellow Texans had hoped for.

14

MIRABEAU BUONAPARTE LAMAR:

Ex-President, Soldier, Diplomat

The Santa Fe Expedition was, unfortunately, like too many things about President Mirabeau Lamar's term in office. Houston had been right in claiming that Lamar was a visionary and completely lacked practicality. When he took office the debt of the young Republic had been about $1 million. At the end of his term the debt was about $7 million, and partially as a result Texas debt paper was worth about 15 cents on the dollar. As an administrator he proved to be a failure. As a visionary, however, he succeeded in at least one area, and because of this he is often called the founder of education in Texas. And although few realize his role in picking its location, Austin is thought of as a nice location for the capital as well as for one of the two universities that his vision also provided for.

After his Presidency, Lamar again had time to work on his still unfinished history of Texas. He collected historical stories and information, including a great deal of information about the exploits of Jean Lafite on Galveston Island. In doing the research for his history book, Lamar interviewed just about all the members of the community who had played some part in the early days and the formation of Texas. These stories were transcribed and several chapters were written, but he still did not find time to complete his book on the history of Texas.

Like the country of Texas, Lamar was rich in land but poor in cash. In April of 1840, he requested that T. G. Gordon help him sell his slaves Emily, Caroline, and a child. In Houston, Gordon was able to get an offer of $2700, $1500 of which was to be used to pay off notes for a carriage to a man named Hall, and the remainder was to be paid "in groceries at the lowest cash price in Houston."

His land holdings included tracts in Grayson, Cherokee, and Smith counties, in addition to Richmond, Texas, where he established his home. To finish the construction of his house, he borrowed $2,000 from his cousin Gazaway Bugg Lamar, who could afford such a loan with ease. The eventual repayment of that loan was to take longer than either one of them probably ever expected. Evidence of this debt appears in a letter dated March 31, 1840 from Gazaway Bugg Lamar, writing from Savannah:

> Dear Cousin,
>
> I received yours 27th Ulto. by mail from New Orleans, yesterday. If Mr. Watrous visits this city I shall be glad to see him. I sent you some 18 or 20 months ago, some land Script issued at New Orleans, for 1600 acres Land to get it located but you never condescended to say one word about that, or any of the letters I have written you.
>
> I shall therefore improve the present occasion when you are an applicant to bring you to remember me. When you give me a reply to that matter stating that the Lands are already located, or that you will positively have them located (provided you can do so conformably to law) you may draw on Geo. W. Lamar, Augusta, Geo. at 60 days for $2000 for my account.
>
> I wish you to draw on him rather than me because I shall be absent after the 1st of May till Nov. next . . . For this loan you may send me your note payable the 1st of January next with interest at 8 prct . . .

The letter continued with political advice, on dealing with Mexico, the need for taxes rather than borrowing, and concludes "Avoid

Loans as far as you can, they are full of pestilence to the people."
Mirabeau really needed the money, as the bill collectors were knocking at the door. On April 7, 1840, Charles DeMorse sent a notice
regarding a note of Mirabeau's that had been placed with DeMorse
by one James H. Smith for collection.

Gazaway's banker's ways were apparently not the manner in
which Mirabeau was accustomed to doing business. He proceeded
to borrow the money from Cousin Gazaway but didn't bother
with some of the details that "Gaz" Lamar had requested. In a
September 1840 letter from Alexandria, Virginia, Gazaway's tone
is frosty: "My Dear Sir; I have nothing from you in reply to my
letter of last Spring. But I am advised that your Draft on Geo. W.
Lamar, drawn to be paid by me, as a loan to you has been accepted, and I shall provide for its payment accordingly. I should
like to hear where my 1600 acres Land are located and get the
Titles by some safe conveyance . . ."

Gazaway goes on to discuss the growing population of Texas,
and its effect on land values, foreign loans for the government, the
need for taxes, and then turns to a more personal note. "You are
aware that I have been married again and have a daughter by my
present wife. My son (Charles A.L. Lamar) is 16 years of age and
well grown and at school in this city. When at Washington and
travelling North last year I met and became partially acquainted
with the Texian Minister Gen. Dunlap who the past summer married a Miss Winn of Washington City, a very elegant and accom-
plished young lady of high respectability and connections and a
friend of my present wife. . . ." The letter ended with a request
that the sojourn in Texas of his wife's friend be made as agreeable
as possible.

During Mirabeau's term in office, his young daughter had
lived with him in Texas, but she longed to return to Georgia where
she had been raised and where the rest of the family lived. After
her father's term as President, she moved to Macon with family
members, and Mirabeau went to visit her in 1843. Upon his return to Texas he was no doubt shocked and saddened to learn of

her death at age 16, possibly an after-effect of the yellow fever she had contracted at Galveston. Always the poet, at that very sad point in his life he penned "On The Death of My Daughter."

In 1846, eight months before he was to go into active service in the Mexican War, Lamar made a gift of the sword that he so highly treasured to Barnard Bee, the son of an old friend.

> My Dear Young Friend—
> Having in my possession a Sword which has long been sheathed in idleness and which is likely to remain so while in my custody, I beg leave to present it to you, not only because you are the son of my warm, personal and political friend, but because I believe it will, in your hands prove more efficient in the service of my country, and more glorious to its wearer. I have preserved it as a cherished relic, for the reason that I placed it at my side for the first time when voluntarily called upon to command a corps on the memorable occasion of giving welcome to the glorious LaFayette in my native state; and I continued to wear it so long as I had the honor of guiding that corps in the defense of the noblest principles of the noblest man of Georgia—George M. Troup. It having been consecrated to such high duties, I could not bear that it should fall into hands which might apply it to ignoble uses . . .

Mexico was still claiming Texas, and no treaty between those countries had been concluded. The annexation of Texas by the United States was the last straw in the eyes of the Mexicans, and war soon broke out with the United States. The aging but eager Mirabeau Lamar organized 67 volunteers who were called into service in October of 1846, and joined Zachary Taylor at Matamoros. After Lamar's appointment as Inspector-General, he was promoted to Lt. Colonel and received a commendation at Monterey.

His money worries continued. Gazaway B. Lamar, writing from Brooklyn in May of 1846, tried to calm his fears:

> By letter I received today from my sister Rebecca I learn that
> between you and Gen McLoed there is some misconcep-
> tion of what I wrote to her, or what he has written to you
> relative to the $1200 I sent you from Savannah and that
> you were pressing and sacrificing the sales of your lands to
> repay it.
>
> To begin, I never wrote anything in any way calling for the
> repayment-my letter alluded entirely to the liens which you
> were to have placed in my hands prior to the loan . . . I took
> occasion to scold you for not only neglecting both, but that
> you had not sent me so much of an acknowledgment of the
> debt by which I could prove it in case of death.
>
> I hope you have secured the Titles to my lands . . .

The letter goes on mention General Tyler's army and that Congress had declared quasi-war, finishing with: "I meant this $1200
as an accommodation to keep you and old Houston apart and if it
has been used otherwise I regret it for that reason."

In 1849 Lamar returned to Georgia on a business trip. This
trip was reported to be in regard to an eleven-league grant of land
to a Georgia company, possibly related to the $6,000 that Lamar
had brought with him upon his return to Texas in 1836.

In 1851 Mirabeau Buonaparte Lamar married Henrietta
Maffitt, age 24 (he was 53), whom he had met at the home of
friends in New Orleans. His bride was the sister of John Newland
Maffitt, who was also the friend of and sometime technical advisor
to Charles A.L. Lamar.

The next year a daughter, Loretto Evalina, named for two of
Mirabeau Lamar's sisters, was born in Macon. This new family
responsibility, along with the need to repay his debt to cousin
Gazaway Bugg Lamar, had put Mirabeau in something of an even
worse financial bind. The solution that he sought was to join the
diplomatic service of the United States. In the summer of 1857,
M. B. Lamar, with the help of friends and relatives in the United
States government, was appointed Minister to the Argentine Re-

public. The salary was less than his poor financial condition required and less than the amount he had hoped for. So, he wrote to Howell Cobb, then the United States Secretary of Treasury, that he wished to delay starting that job because he needed more time to settle "tangled pecuniary affairs." The extent of those tangled affairs is reflected in another letter to cousin Gazaway, dated July 19, 1857.

> Dear gaz,
>
> I have just received the appointment of Minister to the Argentine Confederation, which I am extremely desirous to accept; but which I will not be able to do, unless I can make some arrangements with my creditors, among whom you are the most considerable. I wish, therefore to propose you to receive Lands in payment for what I owe you . . . (you may choose) out of any that I own (except my farm, which I am desirous to retain until I can get a proper fence for it) and at a valuation which shall secure you from the possibility of loss . . .
>
> As a matter of course, I have no right to require any friend to incur risk or hazard of pecuniary loss on my account: I do not mean you to do it: but where a favor can be extended which will relieve the recipient from great embarrassment and mental distress, without inflicting the slightest injury to him who grants it, I think there can be no impropriety in soliciting it. Whatever is done, must be done quickly, as I shall have to accept or decline the appointment of Minister without much further delay.

Old "Gaz" wanted no part of the swap of debt for land. He and Mirabeau finally arranged a suitable settlement, as stated in a letter from "Gaz" sent from Savannah, and dated October 26, 1857: "Dear Cousin, I have yours 18th. Rec'd this morn. from Savannah. I telegraph you to go ahead and arrange my debt by the payment to me as you propose of $1,000 annually from your salary till I am fully paid . . . for which purpose leave with Mr. Cobb the necessary documents in my favor . . . and of course I expect you to go off, angry with me, because I need my monny . . ."

The delay in accepting the job, in spite of the fact that the salary didn't start until the work did, turned out in the long run to be in Lamar's benefit. Just before he was to take the Argentine job, word came that he could be Minister to Nicaragua, and since the arrangement also called for him to be Minister to Costa Rica, the salary was higher, a princely total of $10,000 a year. On December 23, 1857, Lewis Cass, Secretary of State, informed Mirabeau Lamar of his appointment as Envoy Extraordinary and Minister Plenipotentiary to Nicaragua. The notice of the appointment to Costa Rica came on January 20, 1858. At age 59 this appointment finally brought some financial stability to his affairs.

After Christmas of 1857, Lamar set out for Central America, and there he was able to work on several treaties, mostly dealing with cross-isthmus transportation which was of great importance in those days before the Panama Canal. By September of 1859 he had returned to Washington with the job over, and upon completion of his business there returned to Texas. He was at his home in Richmond for the Christmas holiday when on December 19 he complained of not feeling well. The Doctor was called, but as the aging warrior of San Jacinto lay in bed he could only say "I feel very queerly, I believe I am going to die." He was, unfortunately, all too correct: he had suffered a massive and fatal heart attack.

His book on the history of Texas was still unfinished, but his papers and notes proved to be a treasure-trove for later scholars. When published in the 1920s, these papers required six printed volumes. His place in Texas history was permanently established, and he is widely known as the Father of Texas Education. In his honor Texas named Lamar County as well as Lamar University after him.

15

JOSEPH RUCKER LAMAR:

Golf Course to Supreme Court

Joseph Rucker Lamar left his mark in the annals of history as a legal scholar whose career culminated in his appointment to the Supreme Court of the United States of America. The second Lamar to be appointed to that Court, Joseph was the son of James Sanford Lamar and Mary Rucker, both of well known and well established Georgia families. The Ruckers were known to have been in Virginia prior to 1732 and were early Georgia settlers. Mary's father, Joseph Rucker, was the considered to be the lord of his plantations and thus was widely known as "Squire" Rucker. The senior Lamar was a minister, but he had first been trained as a lawyer—quite a combination! After completing his legal training, James Lamar was caught up in a great religious fervor that swept the country, and he became a follower of the Reverend Alexander Campbell. Another follower of Reverend Campbell was Mrs. Richard Tubman, a wealthy society lady. She was impressed by young James Lamar and financed his religious education at Reverend Campbell's Bethany College in Bethany, Virginia (now West Virginia). After college he was to have a lifelong affiliation with the Church of the Disciples in Augusta, Georgia.

Justice Lamar was not a public figure on the national level until his appointment to the highest court in the land. He was, from all that we find in the record, a good, honest family man and lawyer. His life story lacks the drama of blockade running and other activities that some other illustrious members of the Lamar family experienced. Even the other noted Lamar and fellow Supreme Court Justice, Lucius Quintus Cincinnatus Lamar, had several difficult and genuinely harrowing moments during the war as well as legislative battles and triumphs that make for interesting reading. But Joseph Rucker Lamar, who was a young child during the Civil War, and had no direct experience in that great conflict. Apparently he had few other exciting activities that made it into the public record. He went on to marry the daughter of the president of his college, and he remained married to her all his life. Joseph Rucker Lamar went on to be a fine jurist and legal scholar who had the good sense to play golf with President-elect Taft while Taft visited Augusta after he won the election in 1908. Any golfer who seeks justification for the need to play the game (most likely to be offered to a non-golfing spouse) will want to store away in memory the outcome of that meeting on the golf course.

Named after his grandfather, Joseph Rucker Lamar was born in 1857 at Cedar Grove, the Squire's home plantation in Ruckerville, Georgia. His mother had died during the final year of the war, and James Lamar took little Joseph and his brother Philip to Burch Place, a remote plantation owned by their Grandfather Rucker, to keep them out of harm's way as the war wound to an end. In later years Joseph Rucker Lamar remembered his father trying to make Christmas presents. The blockade had cut off the import of all toys, so James Lamar unraveled socks to get yarn from which makeshift balls were made. Another memory was of his father calling all the slaves together to read them the Emancipation Proclamation. Growing up in Augusta, Joseph Rucker Lamar attended Richmond Academy, which is said to be the oldest educational institution in Georgia. He became a friend of Thomas Wilson, a classmate and neighbor who in later years went by his middle name, Woodrow. After the Wilsons moved to South Carolina, many years would pass before Lamar and Wilson would meet again.

After two years at the University of Georgia, Joseph dropped out due an illness. Later, he and his brother Philip went on to finish their undergraduate work at their father's alma mater, Bethany College. Their father had taken a brief transfer to Louisville, claiming to want them near his sons. Considering that the nearest train station was seven rough miles and a two-hour coach ride away, it seems more reasonable that their father may have wanted them exposed to a good religious education. Joseph ignored mathematics and loved Latin, which he read with ease. Another love was baseball. His father wrote, "The boys are juniors at Bethany College—Joe knowing pretty much everything outside the course, and Phil pretty much everything in it. Together they make a good team. Joe has a great deal of the positive in his character, thinks for himself, and generally thinks very soundly and safely. Phil has more respect for the traditions of society, and feels a little surer of his convictions if he has somebody to agree with him." After graduation, Joseph briefly studied law at Washington and Lee but left prior to graduating and went to work for a well-known Augusta lawyer, Henry Clay Foster. As was the common practice in those days, young lawyers learned from their established brethren. When ready to attempt to pass the bar they were required to sit before a judge and answer questions about the law. Foster was a good teacher, and Lamar proved to be a good student who passed the bar in his early twenties.

Following Campbell as President of Bethany College was Dr. Pendleton, another lawyer by training who had fallen under the influence of Reverend Campbell. President Pendleton had a daughter, Clarinda Huntington Pendleton, about whom it was said that she was as smart as she was pretty. She and Joseph. Lamar married, and the next year he was a Latin teacher at Bethany. During that time they lived in the Pendleton house, where it was the standard practice for somebody to be reading aloud at almost all hours of the day. Joseph claimed that the family had become used to the reading out loud almost as background noise. To test his belief, one day while reading he alternated paragraphs from one column then another. After a half hour of this with nobody the wiser, he claimed his theory to be proven correct. The family quickly responded with the claim that they were only being polite to a new member, and thus another family yarn was born.

Upon the offer of a partnership with his legal mentor, Henry Clay Foster, J. R. Lamar moved his family back to Augusta. There they bought a house in the Sand Hills, at 1209 Greene Street, where they lived for many years. The law partnership lasted several years, until the death of the senior partner. After that Lamar was elected to the lower house of the Georgia legislature. An honest man with a good sense of humor and a charming way of making little of himself, he disliked the rough and tumble of campaigning. Swearing that he would never run for office again, he did so only when unopposed. In fact, upon returning to Augusta at the end of the 1886—87 session, he discovered that friends had placed an ad in the paper saying that he was "away from home and had declined to run but it was hoped he would serve if elected." Unopposed, he won and served. He authored legislation that provided for improved administration of the legal process. Based partly on this experience, the state Supreme Court and the Governor chose him to be a commissioner charged with rewriting the state's laws. The revised Civil Code was largely his work, and in those instances where he found problem areas in the law he worked closely with the legislature to pass curative laws.

Research into the history of Georgia's laws led him to London to study the state's colonial legal history. The product of that study was an essay titled "The Bench and Bar of Georgia during the Eighteenth Century," which was followed by "Georgia's Contribution to Law Reform," "A Century's Progress in Law," "Work and Position of the American Court," "A History of the Organization of the Supreme Court," "Life of Judge Nesbet," "Georgia's Law Books," and "A Sketch of Howell Cobb."

Lamar also did a great deal of research on James Oglethorpe that would most likely have been turned into a book had he lived longer. In response to an 1892 speech he gave to the Georgia Bar Association, he received a letter from L.Q.C. Lamar in which his august relative stated that

> I have also read with more pleasure than I can express, your
> paper before the Georgia Bar Association on Georgia's Con-
> tribution to Law Reform. I can see in nearly every line of it
> the movement of a powerful, thoroughly informed and
> well disciplined intellect. It has been an edifying study to
> my own mind; although, when I was a young man, just
> beginning to practice, I had received a lasting impression of
> the judiciary Act of Georgia, in 1799, had preceded, by a
> long period, Lord Brougham's great efforts for Law Reform
> in England . . . yet not until I read your lecture has this
> impression been made so distinct and intelligible. It only
> confirms, however, the pride that I have always had in you
> from your boyhood up to the present moment. The Lamars
> of Georgia were always men of marked character. In the
> early days, when they were at the zenith of their popularity
> and influence, they were remarkable for their probity, frank-
> ness, hospitality, and that sort of rugged courage which
> always made its way and its impress upon newly formed
> communities . . .

In 1903 Joseph Rucker Lamar was appointed to the Georgia Supreme Court, which his wife later stated had been one of her
husband's cherished ambitions. In spite of it having been his am-
bition, he was only there for two years, and by 1905 he was ready
to go back to Augusta and the more lucrative private practice.
Then, as now, private practice was more financially rewarding than
a judgeship, and Lamar joined in partnership with former superior court judge E.H. Callaway. An insight to his method of work
while on the bench is offered by an article that appeared in *The
Savannah Morning News* in 1909 where it was reported that "Judge
Lamar was at his best and held the attention of the Court and
spectators with his splendid conception of the law as it related to
the case. Above Judge Lamar's logic and his law, however, was the
impression created by his delivery of the address to the Court.
Technicalities seemed to fall away from the statutes at his com-

ment and gesture, and the language of the law became very beautiful in his expression of it."

The record books tell us that of all the cases he handled, one in particular was important both personally to Lamar and from a historical legal point of view. In *The Central of Georgia Railway Company v. Wright*, 207 U.S. 127 (1907) Lamar's logic was upheld when the United States Supreme Court overturned the lower court's ruling. After years of allowing no tax to be paid on stock of out-of-state corporations, Georgia not only started taxing these shares but attempted to collect the tax for the previous twenty-five years. On top of that, they demanded interest. Lamar stated

> For 129 years Georgia has been a state, and during all of that long period not one of her citizens has paid taxes on foreign stock. Once, in 1876, an effort was made to collect such a tax. But it failed . . . because of the positive and authoritative ruling by this Court that such stock was a mere symbol and not taxable.
>
> For a quarter of a century citizens and Comptroller alike continued the ancient practice and acquiesced in this ruling, when, in December 1904 the Supreme Court of the United States decided that foreign stock was taxable in Georgia. Armed with this decision the Comptroller reached back through all the years during which this company had rested on the security of the universal practice and the opinion of the Supreme Court of Georgia, and assessed the Georgia Railroad on stock which, up to that time had been universally treated as non-taxable. He did more. He not only assessed it for $126,000 for principal tax, but added interest to such an extent that it nearly equaled the crushing tax itself. But this was not the worst. These extraordinary assessments were made ex parte, without a hearing, without evidence, without trial.

The Supreme Court of the United States has a reputation for not getting involved with issues concerning a state's right to tax. In this case, however, Lamar built his argument on the then-novel approach that the Fourteenth Amendment guarantees due process and that due process had been denied in this instance. After losing at the state level, the law suit was won at the Supreme Court of the United States, a victory that would be remembered when it came time to consider Lamar for the highest court in the land.

In the fall of 1908 President-elect Taft and his family arrived in the Sand Hills area. The previous summer at Hot Springs, Virginia, the Tafts had met a Mrs. Landon Thomas from Augusta and briefly stayed at her Augusta home before leasing one for their own use. Sand Hills was highly suitable, since the nearby Bon Air hotel offered both a golf course and lodging for the President-elect's guests. The next year when Taft returned to Augusta, he paid a visit to the Lamars at their home. The President's aide—and Augusta native—Captain Archie Butt was present that day, and it was his responsibility to keep the President on schedule. At the start of the meeting, he nervously asked Mrs. Lamar if the hall clock kept correct time; she assured him that it did. After a lengthy visit, the President's party left. It was only after they had all gone that Mrs. Lamar noticed that the clock was stopped, and she remembered that she had stopped it to correct the time and had forgotten to start it again. This was the very same clock that Captain Butt had attempted to use to keep the President on schedule. The story was often told within the family and joked about as an example of Mrs. Lamar's control over just about any situation.

During Taft's Presidency two openings came up on the Supreme Court. Although Taft was a Republican and Lamar a Democrat, the President remembered his Georgia friend with whom he had played golf and planned initially on appointing Lamar to the Commerce Court. While discussing his potential choice with Georgia's Senator Augustus Bacon, the President was advised instead that Lamar was a strong legal scholar and worthy of being appointed to the Supreme Court. After asking several other trusted advisors about his golfing friend, the President was sufficiently convinced of J.R. Lamar's legal ability to appoint him to the highest court in the land.

In Washington the Lamars first stayed at the Shoreham Hotel and later moved to 2419 Massachusetts Avenue, which at that time was the last house on the avenue. Later they bought a house at the corner of New Hampshire and S streets. Life in the nation's capital was very different than the life they had lived in Georgia. Almost every night they went out to a dinner party. Invitations were constantly received for events four weeks in advance. This was quite a hub-bub for J. R. Lamar, who had found Atlanta to be such a busy place that he had once commented that if anything bad happened to someone living there, they had to be guilty of contributory negligence (note: a lawyer's attempt at making a joke!). The family quickly rose to the demands of life in Washington and learned to enjoy a busy social life that included dinners at the White House. On one unforgettable night they shared a box at the opera with the Tafts. The event was a breath-taking experience, because the start of the performance was delayed pending the arrival of the President. As soon as the Presidential party entered the box, the band started playing the national anthem and all eyes in the house were on the Presidential box. The startled Justice & Mrs. Joseph Rucker Lamar suddenly found themselves in the spotlight standing alongside the President.

Recognition of his work on the Court followed when in 1911 Yale University awarded him an honorary Doctorate of Law, and the Lamars enjoyed a visit to the campus in New Haven for commencement. The next year they received the sad news about the sinking of the *Titanic*, on which their friend and former Presidential aide Archie Butts was lost. When Wilson defeated President Taft (and Teddy Roosevelt) in 1912, Joseph Lamar wrote to congratulate the New Jersey Governor. The response came back: "My Dear Justice Lamar: It is hard for me to begin this letter without saying My Dear Joe, so vividly do I remember when you and Philip and I played together . . ."

Among Lamars friends and supporters were one or more members of the Society of Cincinnati, which had been founded by officers in Washington's Continental Army and which offered membership only to their direct descendants. Although several Lamars were members or at least eligible to be members, J.R. Lamar's antecedents do not seem to have been among them. His friends nonetheless made him an honorary member of the Georgia chapter of the Society in 1913.

At the White House reception after Wilson's inauguration the Lamars met Mrs. Wilson, who greeted them cordially and commented that of the few people that her husband knew in Washington, two were Justices. Mrs. Lamar was standing near a side door when the President quietly entered. Upon hearing her name, the President immediately asked to talk with her husband. The two greeted as old friends and immediately recalled experiences and swapped stories of their Georgia youth.

In 1914 President Wilson appointed Lamar to head a three-man delegation to end a diplomatic crisis with Mexico that had come about because Wilson had refused to recognize Huerta as president of Mexico. Huerta's actions had caused such an outcry that the Senate passed a resolution allowing the use of armed force against Mexico. Because Lamar showed great tact and ability in resolving the matter, Wilson wished to appoint him as a delegate to the Pan-American Conference, but J. R. Lamar declined, fearing that to accept would cause him to be away from the Court too long. When the First World War broke out in Europe, Lamar was not in agreement with the camp that wanted the United States to remain neutral. German demands for free passage of their armies through neutral Belgium outraged him. He conferred with the President often and supported a strong stand against Germany.

Age and the stress of the job were taking their toll. On a trip to White Sulfur Springs, Justice Lamar experienced pain and difficulty raising his left arm. The doctors soon diagnosed an enlargement of the heart and high blood pressure. The Lamars returned to Washington, where the Justice recovered some of his mobility, although he required a cane for walking. He was still suffering from the effects of the earlier stroke when in January of 1916 his heart problems became too much for him. He died in his 59th year, leaving his widow and two sons, Philip Rucker Lamar and William Pendleton Lamar. He is buried in the Sand Hills area of Augusta, Georgia.

Lord Bryce, who had been the British Ambassador to the United States, wrote to Mrs. Lamar, "Your husband was one of the friends whom we most valued in Washington, and I recall with a pleasure now darkened by sadness the many conversations we had together and all that I learnt from him. He seemed to me to have an eminently just and wide mind, always seeking for the truth in a spirit of perfect candour and penetrating deep to the true reasons of political principle and legal rules. It was a privilege to know him, and I deeply mourn for your Country as well as yourself and those others who were nearest to him, his withdrawal from the high post which he adorned."

From President Wilson came these words: "My heartfelt sympathy goes out to you on your tragic loss, which the whole country has reason to mourn. It has lost an able and noble servant. I have lost in him one of my most loved friends."

G

16

SEVERAL OTHER LAMARS:

Historical Notes

Many other Lamars have served in the Congress of the United States or show up in records in the service of their country. Like their illustrious kin, most are men of the nineteenth and early twentieth centuries.

Henry Graybill Lamar was born in Clinton, Georgia, in 1798 and became a judge of the state Superior Court. Later, Henry Graybill was in the Georgia state House of Representatives and served in the United States Congress. Having been elected as a Jeffersonian, he represented Georgia from December 1829 until March 1833. As such, he was one of the persons appointed to accompany the Marquis de Lafayette on his arrival to Georgia. After that he lost his bid for re-election, and he later made an unsuccessful run for Governor. He died in September of 1861 and is buried in Macon, Georgia.

James Robert Lamar was born in Edgar Springs, Missouri, in 1866, and started out as a school teacher. He later was appointed principal of Licking Academy in Missouri. Following his academic career, he studied law and was admitted to the bar of Texas County, Missouri, in 1889. He represented Missouri in the United States Congress from 1903 to 1905. After his death he was buried in Houston, Missouri.

William Harmong Lamar, a lawyer from Alabama, married L.Q.C. Lamar's daughter, Virginia Longstreet Lamar. They lived in Washington, where he was appointed Associate Solicitor General by Woodrow Wilson. Both he and his wife shared a keen interest in family origins, and they bought property in Rockville, Maryland, which they claimed was part of a property owned by the first Thomas. (In 1996 Howard Robert Lamar, retired history professor and acting president of Yale University, wondered whether this property could have been at or near Hunting Hill.)

John Basil Lamar, was born in Milledgeville, Georgia, in November 1812, and attended Franklin College (now the University of Georgia). John Basil represented his state in the 28th United States Congress from March to July 1843, when he resigned. It is possible that his very extensive plantation holdings required his direct management. Prior to the outbreak of the Civil War, he was a delegate to the state convention that adopted Georgia's secession ordinance in 1861. He saw action in the Civil War as an aide on the staff of General Howell Cobb (formerly a Georgia Congressman and Speaker of the House whose wife was Mary Ann Lamar). John Basil Lamar fought and was fatally wounded at the battle at Crampton's Gap. He died the next day. He is buried at Macon, Georgia.

L.Q.C. Lamar's younger brother, Jefferson Mirabeau Lamar, also died in this battle. Cobb's forces had been brought into the battle late in the day in a last-ditch attempt to hold the strategic pass through which passed a road from Frederick, Maryland, to Harpers Ferry. Federal troops were already pushing the remnants of the vastly outnumbered Confederates through the gap when Cobb's men arrived. Upon receiving the order to hold a position to the right side of a field, Jefferson Lamar found that the enemy was already dug in behind a stone wall. He immediately ordered a charge and led his men over the wall. As the horse and rider flew over the wall, a deadly hail of gunfire cut the animal from beneath Lamar. Climbing to his feet in an attempt to rally his men, he met the same fate as his horse. This battle was extremely bloody in relation its size. Over half of Cobb's forces were wiped out in a few hours. This fighting, referred to as the battle for South Mountain, was took place while the armies were maneuvering for position in a prelude to what became known to the North as the battle of Antietam and to the South as Sharpsburg.

William Bailey Lamar, who was born near Monticello, Jefferson County, Florida, not far from Tallahassee, in 1863. From 1866 to 1873 he lived in Athens, Georgia, home of the University of Georgia, where he went to college. He received his law degree from Lebanon Law School in Lebanon, Tennessee. This nephew of L.Q.C. Lamar practiced law in Tupelo, Mississippi, and then went to Florida, where he was a judge from 1883 to 1886. Next followed a term in the Florida House of Representatives. From 1889 to 1903 William Bailey Lamar was Attorney General of Florida, after which he served in the United States Congress from 1903 to 1909. He died at his winter home at Thomasville, Georgia, and is buried in Athens, Georgia.

Thomas Gresham Lamar was in charge of a Civil War earthwork fort defending the approach to Charleston, South Carolina. The men under his leadership fought bravely to hold their bloody ground and won the Battle of Sessionville. Their leader, however, was mortally wounded and died in Charleston. He was promoted to General posthumously, and the fort he died defending was named in his honor—Fort Lamar. He is buried at Magnolia Cemetery, Augusta, Georgia. The battle has been re-enacted for several years (in the 1990s) at Boone Hall Plantation in Mt. Pleasant, S.C.

Research conducted by Ruth Hunter (aunt of the author of this volume), who had been a lawyer in Washington, states that "By consulting various government records, it is noted that several of the Lamars rendered important services in the Revolutionary War, War of 1812, and Civil War."

In these papers, Hunter mentions a man who, if he is what some written records claim, would be a great mystery of the Revolution. "General" Maximillian Lamar, according to various family documents, was killed in the American Revolution at the Battle of Saratoga. This battle took place early in the Revolution, in 1777, and my correspondence with the Saratoga National Historical Park indicates that they do not list any Maryland Militia as having fought in the battle of Saratoga. *The Politics of Command in the American Revolution* by J.G. Rossie, in which is listed the general staff of the Revolution (77 Major Generals and Brigadier Generals) does not have Maximillian Lamar among them. Copies of articles on the Lamar family that were published in the *Baltimore Sun* in 1905 (and which are on file in the Maryland Historical Society) have several references to "Gen." Maximillian Lamar. One says he was killed at Saratoga. Another says that "among the marriage records of Frederick County can be found that of Mary Ann (Polly) Lamar, daughter of Maximillian Lamar, to Hugh Glover, July 29, 1811 . . ." Another letter responding to and printed by the *Sun* tells who his descendants are.

It is most likely that he was not in fact a General who has been missed by the history books but rather someone who had been given the nickname of General. Extensive research in the Maryland state archives has failed to locate any military or other information about Maximillian Lamar.

Capt. Abraham Lamar was incorrectly identified in some family papers as a member of the Society of Cincinnati (which he was not, according to the society's librarian). Others claim that he was killed at Saratoga, but no proof has been found to support this. He is another one who does not appear in searches of the Maryland state archives.

Major Mareen Lamar was also killed in the Revolution, at Paoli Tavern, in 1777. This is well documented in various books, and Ruth Hunter's notes say that he was buried at St. Davids on September 20, 1777.

Mack Lamar—"no record found" states Hunter's note. It is possible that this could have been another name for Maximillian

William Bishop Lamar of Frederick County, Maryland, is thought to have served in the militia in the Revolution. It has been accepted by the Daughters of the American Revolution that he signed an oath of allegiance. In the final days of his life, on a trip home to Maryland after visiting family who had moved west, William Bishop Lamar was thrown from a horse while crossing through the Cumberland Gap. Soon after the accident he wrote his will and subsequently died. His will is on file in both Tennessee and Maryland. He is buried near where he fell in Hawkins, Tennessee. Another William Lamar, specifically William Lynch Lamar—also from Maryland—served in the Continental Army and was a member of the Society of Cincinnati. He went on to fight in the War of 1812 and was laid to rest in Cumberland, Maryland. His headstone details a long list of the battles that he fought in, including Harlem Heights, White Plains, Staten Island, Camden, Monmouth, Germantown, Guilford Courthouse, and the Siege of Ninety-Six.

Cincinnatus A.L. Lamar is listed as a Captain in the Georgia Militia, 1777. (*Historical Register of Officers of the Continental Army During the war of the Revolution*, 1914)

WORKS CITED

Lucius Quintus Cincinnatus Lamar:

Cate, Wirt A. *Lucius Q. C. Lamar*. University of North Carolina Press, 1935.

Chesnut, Mary B. *A Diary from Dixie*. Houghton Mifflin, 1949.

Kennedy, John F. *Profiles in Courage*. Harper & Bros., 1955.

Mayes, Edward, *Lucius Q. C. Lamar*. Publishing House of the Methodist Episcopal Church (South), 1896.

Murphy, James B. *L.Q.C. Lamar*. Louisiana State University Press, 1973.

Strode, Hudson. *Jefferson Davis: Confederate President*. Harcourt Brace, 1959.

Gazaway Bugg Lamar:

Bradlee, Francis. *Blockade Running During the Civil War*. Essex Institute, 1925.

Carse, Robert. *The Civil War at Sea*. Rinehart, & Co., 1958.

Cochran, Hamilton. *Blockade Runners of the Confederacy*. Bobbs-Merrill Company, Inc., 1958.

Horner, Dave. *The Blockade Runners*. Dodd, Mead & Co., 1968.

Illustrated London News, July 16, 1864.

Mathis Robert Neil. *Gazaway Bugg Lamar: A Southern Entrepreneur*. Dissertation Submitted to the Graduate Faculty of the University of Georgia, 1968.

New York Times, January 28, 1866, and October 10, 1877.

Ross, Malcolm. *The Cape Fear*. Holt, Rinehart and Winston, 1965.

Snow, Edward Rowe. *The Vengeful Sea*. Dodd, Mead and Co., 1956.

Wise, Stephen. *Lifeline of the Confederacy*. University of South Carolina Press, 1988. Stick, David. *Graveyard of the Atlantic*. University of North Carolina Press, 1952.

Charles Augustus Lafayette Lamar:
Henderson, Tom. *The Slave Ship Wanderer*. University of Georgia Press, 1967.
Mannix, Daniel P. *Black Cargoes*. Viking Press, New York, 1962.
Myers, Robert Manson. *The Children of Pride*. Yale University Press, 1972.
The North American Review, November, 1886.

Mirabeau Buonaparte Lamar:
Christian, Asa Kyrus. *M.B. Lamar*. Von Bockman Jones Printers, n.d.
Graham, Philip. *The Life and Poems of Mirabeau B. Lamar*. University of North Carolina Press, 1938.
Gulick, Charles Adams Jr. *The Papers of Mirabeau Buonaparte Lamar*. A.C. Baldwin & Sons, n.d.
Houston, Sam. *Official Report of the Battle of San Jacinto*.
MacIntire, Jean Bacon. *Lafayette, Guest of the Nation*. Anthony J. Simone Press, 1967.
Siegel, Stanley. *The Poet President*. Pemberton Press, 1977.
Tolbert, Frank X. *The Day of San Jacinto*. Pemberton Press, 1959.
Winter, Nevin. *Texas the Marvelous*. The Page Company, 1916.

Joseph Rucker Lamar:
Friedman, Leon and Fred W. Israel. *The Justices of the United States Supreme Court*. Chelsea House, 1969.
Lamar, Clarinda P. *The Life of Joseph Rucker Lamar*. G. P. Putnam's & Sons, 1926.

END NOTES

*Residents of the great State of Texas may understandably feel that Mirabeau Buonaparte Lamar is better known, at least there, since Texas has named a county and a university—as well as main thoroughfares in Houston and other major cities—after their war hero and former president of the Republic of Texas. Nevertheless, Lucius was a widely known public figure who spent more years in public office, held higher positions in national government, and was highly regarded as an orator.

*Author's note: I wonder whether this means that L.Q.C.'s devotion to Constance Cary created no "heartburning" for Mary Chestnut because Lucius was a "freelance" and no longer romantically involved with her?

*Years later, when Lamar was made Secretary of the Interior, Walthall was appointed to fill the Senate seat vacated by Lamar, and Walthall then won the seat in his own name at the next election.

* Sometimes misspelled in history books as *Lillian*

*An Englishman, Tom Taylor, who was the agent for the English owned Confederate Trading Company, had been on board the company-owned *Banshee* on her maiden run into Wilmington early in the war. She had made it safely through New Inlet with the help of the original guns at the fort, which didn't have very great range. Realizing how much more helpful Whitworths would be, Taylor arranged for them as a gift to the fort's commander, Colonel Lamb. The Colonel also salvaged some additional Whitworths from a wrecked blockade runner. Taylor's company could well afford the gift, since Taylor, after *Banshee* had at last been lost, calculated the return on investment the company earned from her eight round trips at 700% of the total investment.

9 780738 824109